VISION & VOICE

Also by Linda Rief

SEEKING DIVERSITY
Language Arts with Adolescents

ALL THAT MATTERS
What Is It We Value in School and Beyond?
edited with Maureen Barbieri

WORKSHOP 6
The Teacher as Writer
edited with Maureen Barbieri

VISION & VOICE
EXTENDING THE LITERACY SPECTRUM

LINDA RIEF

HEINEMANN • Portsmouth, NH

Heinemann

A division of Reed Elsevier Inc.
361 Hanover Street
Portsmouth, NH 03801–3912

Offices and agents throughout the world.

http://www.heinemann.com

We would like to thank those who have given their permission to include material in this book.

Portions of *Weaving the Threads of Response* first published in *Voices from the Middle* NCTE Vol.1 No.1 Sept. 1994

Kirsten's Notecards (Figure 3–15) first published in *Voices from the Middle* NCTE Vol.4 No.4 November 1997

"Bigfoot's Grampa" used with permission from *Keepers of the Earth, Native American Stories and Environmental Activities for Children*, by Michael J. Caduto & Joseph Bruchac. © 1988, 1989, 1997. Fulcrum Publishing, Inc., Golden, CO. All rights reserved.

Songs from *Thread of Life*. Lyrics and musical arrangements © David A. Ervin, Linda Rief, and Joshua Stamper. Reprinted by permission of the authors.

In the accompanying CD:
The Paper Bag Princess by Robert Munsch. Copyright © 1980. Published by Annick Press Ltd. Used by permission of the publisher.

Library of Congress Cataloging-in-Publication Data

Rief, Linda.
    Vision and voice : extending the literacy spectrum / Linda Rief.
      p.   cm.
    Includes bibliographical references.
    ISBN 0-325-00097-2
    1. Language arts (Middle school)—United States.   2. Arts—Study and teaching (Middle school)—United States.   3. Interdisciplinary approach in education—United States.   I. Title.
    LB1631.R536   1998
    428´.0071´2—DC21   98-34180
                                        CIP

Editors: Lois Bridges and Leigh Peake
Production: Renée Le Verrier
Cover design: Darci Mehall/AUREO DESIGN
Cover photo: Keith Whittier, eighth grade, Oyster River Middle School
Multimedia Developer: Dan Breslin
Manufacturing: Louise Richardson

Printed in the United States of America on acid-free paper

02 01 00 99 98   RRD   1 2 3 4 5 6

CONTENTS

● Please explore the accompanying CD for additional samples of student art, text, and voice.

● Please explore the accompanying CD for additional samples of student art, text, and voice.

💿 Please explore the accompanying CD for additional samples of student art, text, and voice.

for
Beth Doran Healey
teacher, artist
and
David A. Ervin
teacher, musician

INTRODUCTION

Einstein admitted that he did not think in words, but visual images. His early formulations for the theory of relativity came in images of himself riding a light wave. Only later did he come to words. (Fueyo, 1991, p. 13)

Vision and Voice is about reading and writing but it is mainly about slowing down. It is about letting students observe and view, interpret, and represent their worlds with more than words. It is about inviting, encouraging, and teaching our students to use visual images, voices, and words to show us how they see the extraordinary in the ordinary and how they make sense of their worlds through all the ways that make sense to them.

On a Tuesday morning, or Thursday, or Friday, I'm in my usual hurry from the mailboxes back to my room for first period class. As I pass the science room I hear a student's voice, "Mrs. Rief! Mrs. Rief!" Seth rushes after me holding a book in his hands. "Mrs. Rief, I'm reading a *mouthwatering book* . . . Just listen to this: A woman once asked John Viehman, 'Why walk?' and he said, 'Because the world looks different at two miles an hour? Because spring comes one flower at a time? Because a mountain reveals itself to those who climb it? Because I like the drama of crags and gullies emerging from behind a curtain of mist and then disappearing again as the fog rolls in and out? Because of the way wind cools the skin and a snowflake stings the tongue?' (p. 11) Isn't that awesome writing?" Seth says. I not only slow down; I stop. "Seth, read that again. 'Because the world looks different at two miles an hour. . . . Because spring comes one flower at a time. . . .' What book is that? That is 'mouthwatering'."

Seth is all smiles. He has finally found a book about something he loves doing—hiking and backpacking—and he is in awe of the way John Viehman uses words to describe his experiences.

Vision and Voice is about helping students see, and represent what they learn, broadly and deeply. It is about extending our notions of the literacy spectrum to include the visual and oral arts in the reading and writing classroom by encouraging students to develop their imaginations as they envision possibilities for their lives and their worlds.

Sketching, painting, drawing, storytelling, reading, writing, singing—slow us down and make us step inside worlds we too often rush past. "Participatory involvement with the many forms of art," says Maxine Greene, "does enable us at the very least, to see more in our experience, to hear more on normally unheard frequencies, to become conscious of what daily routines, habits, and conventions have obscured." (p. 379) I try to teach students to show how they view, think about, and react to the world. If they have ways of doing that beyond words, that's what I want them to use.

How do students en*vision* the world? How do they *voice* what they see and think? Reading, writing, speaking, and listening are at the core of the language arts classroom. *Vision and Voice* is about writing and reading with more than words so that all students can become better writers and readers by becoming close observers and users of language as well. In the context of their own drawings, their own storytellings, their own songs, their own writing, they gain an insider's view of what it means to know. "A writer must see with the painter's eye," says Paul Horgan, "a writer must have an ear for the music of words, the actor's gift of mimicry, the capacity to take any part." (McCullough, 1988, pp. 13 & 16)

Maxine Greene confirms the need to be a participant in a work in order to know it well. "Mere exposure to a work of art is not sufficient to be an aesthetic experience. There must be conscious participation in a work, a going out of energy, an ability to notice what is there to be noticed in the play, the poem, the quartet." (p. 379)

Children come to us with various strengths. Adam and Ethan struggle with writing. But when I encourage Adam to draw or Ethan to slip into character for storytelling or listen to Spencer, the smallest, quietest boy in the class overpower *Ulysses* as he, *Polyphemus*, shouts, "You are a ninny, or else you come from the other side of nowhere, telling *me* mind the gods . . ." I find that meaning they take to and from a text is clearly thoughtful and thorough. Those students who normally do not experience success through the written word often meet their goals through spoken or visual representations of all they know and think.

A PRACTICAL GUIDE

Vision and Voice is meant to be a practical guide for teachers. Two comprehensive research projects form the core of the book. The first is an environmental study of the rain forest that integrates reading, writing, art, science, and math. The second, centered on the textile mills of the Industrial Revolution, connects reading, writing, and music. Neither project is meant to be an end unto itself. The two projects are showcased on the CD included with the book. As you explore the images of the rain forest and listen to some of the songs of a stage production written and directed by students, I hope you will discover, both literally and metaphorically, the visions and voices of adolescents in a language-rich classroom.

Extensive pictures and appendixes take you through each comprehensive project. Appendixes A through G and O, relate to *rain forests.* Appendixes P through W relate to our musical, *Weaving the Threads of Response.*

Appendixes H through N are examples of student work that involve research, reading, writing, and illustrating when the focus is not the rain forest, yet the connections with science are evident. This is by no means an exhaustive list, but may provide enough of a sample to see the many ways in which students can, and do, extend the literacy spectrum.

Appendix I, *The Pond in my Classroom,* is an example of the way one student, Alexis, went about converting factual information into a narrative, introduced the story with another student's perceptions (professionally published literature), and used her talents as an artist (See the CD for Alexis's watercolors) to tell the story.

Appendix J, Current Issues, is based on a topic we may be currently studying, in this case kangaroos in Australia, and polar bears in the Arctic. These are two examples of *informed* opinions. Katie and John, respectively, use various viewpoints from their reading to reach their own conclusions.

Appendix K: Judy George and Janet Martell, sixth- and seventh-grade teachers at Oyster River Middle School, introduced me to the concept of an Ecology Anthology as an alternative to the school newspaper. In this particular case, we visited a local buffalo farm to begin our studies of endangered plants and animals of North America. Students used photos and cartoons to enhance their hard news, feature stories, and op-ed pieces. Groups of students were responsible for various pages in this combined publication. There are three pages included here to give a sense of the Ecology Anthology. (The instructions for this anthology are given to students on a handout, Appendix H.)

Appendix L, is an example of all Nika learned and presented about Vision Defects, written and illustrated as a pamphlet Sue Bissell, a science teacher, often invites students to create innovative presentations of particular studies.

Appendix M is a children's picture book. While studying tidal pools along the seacost of Maine and New Hampshire, Kelly *Orange is the Starfish*, shared here without the colored illustrations or in the bound format. It was submitted for both science and language arts requirements.

Appendix N is a pamphlet in which Troy presented his information about dog whelks after choosing the organism as part of their tidal pool studies in science class.

If we expand the meaning-making options in our classrooms, our students will respond and show us who they are as learners and as human beings. My hope is that these materials provide samples that inform and inspire other students, and that the appendixes give a framework for shaping the processes of your own studies. The numerous samples are meant to show the impressive work students do when given such a variety of opportunities to show all they know. It is the students' work that ultimately moves us and pushes us to delve deeper into new ideas and approaches that keep language alive and fresh for all of us.

In addition, brief, practical vignettes (*Picturing Possibilities* and *Listening to Language*) show how to extend the literacy spectrum to include the visual and oral arts on a day-to-day basis. These possibilities are meant to say: "Here are some small ideas that make big differences for some students. In our fifty-minute classrooms these might be all we can attempt. That's the reality for many of us."

Language Arts

Vision and Voice is about visual and oral opportunities as complements and alternatives—but not as replacements—in a rigorous language arts classroom. It is about language *arts*. I am not an artist, nor am I a musician. I am not trying to teach art or music. I am offering students other ways to construct meaning and communicate understanding of their reading, writing, viewing, and living.

At a National Council of Teachers of English luncheon several years ago, seminal thinker and art educator Elliot Eisner reminded us that imagination, passion, and vision are fundamental to education. They "awaken our sensibilities to things that often pass us by . . . the outcome of a work of art is a surprise to the maker, and in the surprise the work of art remakes the maker. The great function of art is not only to provide another world for others, but to redefine ourselves because we are in the process of entering possibilities, entering worlds, finding things that we didn't know were there when we started." (quoted from luncheon)

In the picture book *i live in music* by Ntozake Shange, the illustrator Romare Bearden writes in the afterword, "I think the artist has to be something like a whale, swimming with his mouth wide open, absorbing everything until he has what he really needs. When he finds that, he can start to make limitations. And then he really begins to grow."

Megan, one of my eighth graders, wrote a two-minute journal entry in response to Bearden's words. Throughout the week, she revised her thoughts again and again until she had crafted a piece of writing.

> Art comes from everything around us. Whether I'm working with a paintbrush, musical notes, or simply words, everything I see, hear, and feel goes into my work. Though it may seem unimportant at the time, things around us become a part of us and influence all that we do.
>
> Many people don't realize the truth in this. Some go through life hurrying from one thing to the next, never taking the time to enjoy life's little pleasures. I make a point of running through leaf piles whenever I see them. I love the crunching noise they make under my feet, the crisp, brittle feeling that they have, the smell that I know can belong to autumn alone.
>
> And what better way is there to spend a warm summer day than on your back watching the clouds drift overhead? I love just relaxing on the soft grass with the sweetness of the breeze and the clouds for company. Letting my mind wander, finding all kinds of creatures in the slow moving whiteness. Sometimes a butterfly

soars by on a puff of wind and I get up to chase after it, following the elusive insect for what seems like hours, until I lose sight of it in a ray of sun.

Maybe one of the greatest little pleasures of all is puddle jumping. So many people forget the joy of stomping in a puddle, when you can still smell the freshness of the rain and the dampness of the air. It's especially fun with friends, because then you can try to soak each other as well as yourself. I love the sound of water sloshing around in my shoes with each step. The feeling of being totally soaked. It's by far one of my favorite things about April.

These sights, sounds, smells, and feelings all become a part of me. Even though I don't realize it sometimes, they all work their way into all that I do, and all that I am. It makes all of my art—writing in particular—seem real. If I can capture the smell of the leaves, the feeling of the sun on my face, the splash of a puddle, I have made my writing come alive. The reader can experience the same feelings that I had on that rainy day in April.

What I'm saying is that we all need to be more like that whale. Absorb things from the world around us. Notice details. Feed on them, use them to grow. Chase butterflies. See how high we can go on swings. Remember the taste of an apple fresh from the tree. Little things. Things that the busy, preoccupied side of each of us doesn't notice. But things that the whale in us does.

Megan discovered things about herself that she didn't know were there before she started thinking and writing. She complained for weeks that she had nothing to write about. Yet, through this piece of writing, she not only provides a convincing example of all that Eisner tells us, but she redefines and surprises herself in the process. Her imagination, passion, and vision awaken our sensibilities to so many of the things that we often pass by. The act of making art—writing, drawing, storytelling, dramatic readings—encourages our students to be awake to possibilities. It's about paying attention to the world through multiple ways of knowing.

"Encounters with art," says Maxine Greene, "nurture and sometimes provoke growth of individuals who reach out to one another as they seek clearings in their experience and try to live more ardently in the world." (p. 381)

Vision and Voice is about paying attention and giving voice to the promises in each of our students. It is about living more ardently in our classrooms, so that we all may live more ardently in the world.

REFERENCES

EISNER, ELLIOT. 1998. *The Kind of Schools We Need.* Portsmouth, NH: Heinemann.

FUEYO, JUDITH A. 1991. "Language Arts Classrooms: Spaces Where Anything Can Happen." *Writing Teacher*, Sept.

GREENE, MAXINE. 1995. "Art and Imagination: Reclaiming the Sense of Possibility." *Phi Delta Kappan*, 76, 378–382.

McCULLOUGH, DAVID. 1988. "Introduction" from *A Writer's Eye* (Paul Horgan). New York: Harry N. Abrams, Inc.

SHANGE, NTOZAKE. 1978. *i live in music*. New York: Welcome Enterprises.

VIEHMAN, JOHN. 1995. *Hiking and Backpacking: A Trailside Series Guide*. New York: Norton

ACKNOWLEDGMENTS

I live in a community of learners. My colleagues and friends constantly keep me reading, rethinking, wondering, and writing about the classroom. Don Murray, Don Graves, Tom Newkirk, Tom Romano, Susan Stires, Cinthia Gannett, Jean Robbins, Doug Kaufman, Nancie Atwell, and especially Maureen Barbieri—their vision and their voices, their passion and their commitment, inspire me as a learner and teacher.

In her book *Authors of Pictures, Draughtsmen of Words*, Ruth Hubbard first helped me recognize how my students made meaning with their drawing. In *Picturing Learning*, Karen Ernst pushed me into sketching for myself. And Joni Chancer and Gina Rester-Zodrow, authors of *Moon Journals*, clearly showed me—and my students—how to look at and represent our worlds more deeply and more carefully with writing that inspires art, and art that inspires writing.

The educators at Oyster River Middle School inspire me every year through their own commitment to seeking the most innovative and productive ways to work with students. Sue Bissell, Michele McInnes, and Mark Nichols, the team of teachers with whom I've been working for several years, continually provide a professional voice, a sounding board, and a wealth of ideas as we meet to work out ideas for curricula development and ways of working with the strengths of diverse students. They are the voices of reason and humor.

Alan Stuart, John MacArthur, and Beth Doran Healey formed the core of teachers with whom I researched, designed, and built the rainforest described in this book. Beth and Alan worked tirelessly for hours after school helping students construct and dismantle the rainforest, then reconstruct it at the Portsmouth Children's Museum in Portsmouth, New Hampshire.

Thread of Life is only one of the musicals Dave Ervin and I have produced together over the years. Some were better than others, but the important point is understanding the processes that students go through to grow as learners. Dave has taught me how to look for, and encourage, the different strengths in children. Because of Dave's expertise, students come from music classes singing, humming, and smiling.

Joshua Stamper, a high school student at the time, and Maggie Moore, my intern, also made valuable individual contributions. Peg Higgins supplied many of the annotations for works cited in *Thread of Life*.

Toby Gordon, former editorial director at Heinemann, provided the inspiration to even begin this project. She enthusiastically nudged the telling of what we did, gave the initial draft a thorough read, and asked the essential questions that moved the writing in many directions.

Kelly Eggers, director of Oyster River Players, an amateur theater group for children and adults, draws from children the promises we seldom see or value in the classroom. She makes me realize how much kids are capable of when we nurture their strengths. She has taught me how to help students use their voices as readers and storytellers.

This has been the most complicated *writing* project I have ever undertaken. Without the expertise and technical skills of the editorial and production team at Heinemann, I would not have had the confidence to carry through with all the complex details, particularly those involved by including a compact disk with visual and auditory functions. Lois Bridges, my editor, carefully read and tightened up my words. Her patience and trust in me as a writer, and her excitement over what the students had done, was enough of an invitation to keep me writing. Leigh Peake, editorial director and technology wizard, provided the know-how to produce the CD. Renée Le Verrier, managing editor, and my production editor, framed the entire project with her thorough reading of the manuscript and detailed vision for the CD. Mike Gibbons, general manager, was always available to listen in order the keep the book moving forward. Many thanks to Lois, Leigh, Renée, and Mike for making something so complicated look so easy.

Finally, many, many thanks to all the seventh and eighth grade students over the years who have shown me, and now show others, all they know and can do through their vision of the world and through their voices as they represent and celebrate their lives and learning.

REFERENCES

CHANCER, JONI and GINA RESTER-ZODROW. 1997. *Moon Journals: Writing, Art, and Inquiry*. Portsmouth, NH: Heinemann.

ERNST, KAREN. 1994. *Picturing Learning: Artists and Writers in the Classroom*. Portsmouth, NH: Heinemann.

HUBBARD, RUTH. 1989. *Authors of Pictures, Draughtsmen of Words*. Portsmouth, NH.: Heinemann.

1 | KEEPING THE *SEARCH* IN RESEARCH

To research is to learn deliberately.
Garth Boomer

Research. The word used to send shivers through me. When I was in school, research meant spending inordinate amounts of time reading encyclopedias and copying volumes of information I cared little about, in a way that didn't look like I had plagiarized it. But I loved decorating covers, drawing flowers next to each page number, and listing pages of references. My teachers loved my reports too. I always received *A*-pluses because I was very good at taking notes and spitting back what someone else had said. I did these reports for the grade only. I didn't care about the information itself. I didn't formulate my own questions, nor did I dig deeply for the answers.

Outside of school, it was a different story. I remember a "travel club" that Pam, Anne, and I founded when we were in seventh grade. No one else belonged and we never solicited additional members. We planned our future trips. We rode our bikes downtown and collected all the brochures the local travel agent was willing to give us. Small notepads in hand, we interviewed travel agents, parents, neighbors. We made lists of where we wanted to go (Hawaii, Mexico, Japan, Finland . . .), how long we wanted to stay, what we would do there, what we needed to take. We made lists of questions: What do we know about each place? Why do we want to go there? When's the best time to travel? What do we want to see when we get there? The actual cost of such exotic travel never hindered our plans.

We created jobs for each club member: president, secretary, treasurer. We assigned tasks to each job and had folders to store "important documents" connected to each position. We collected dues (ten cents a week) from all our members. We spent the entire summer researching far away places. In the end, our big trip was winning permission from our parents to take the bus to Quincy (the biggest city near our small town), two towns away, to shop at the Bargain Center (we had listed all the stores and asked which ones had the best prices) by ourselves. Our purchases weren't so important. Dividing the money collected in dues (enough to cover bus fare for the three of us), reading the bus schedule, riding out of our small town, and searching through the bins of bargain sweaters, socks, and underwear, our pocketbooks slung over our shoulders (all without parents) was travel at its best. We were ready because we had researched our trip.

FREE CHOICE—AND PARAMETERS

Today, I want my students to approach research with the same passion that my friends and I researched our trips. When my son Bryan was in seventh grade, his social studies teacher assigned him the topic, "cooking utensils of the Colonial Period" for his six-week research project. Bryan was not even mildly enthused. My daily badgering only reminded him how much he hated the topic. I dragged him to the library and I flipped through card catalogs while he sauntered off to look at *Sports Illustrated*. I even remember reading through the eventual stack of books myself, putting tags on the right spots where he would find information, laying out index cards for him, and bribing him to gather notes. It wasn't until we stopped in at a local antique shop and found a few authentic cooking utensils that Bryan finally became motivated enough to begin gathering notes. When Bryan began fingering those ladles, spoons, and odd shaped pans, it sparked his interest. He talked to the antique dealer. We visited a local museum and he questioned the tour guides in the Colonial kitchens for additional information. He wanted to know how and why cooking utensils had or had not changed. His questions formed the categories for his report. The answers formed the essence of his discoveries. He organized his notes. He wrote. And he drew. When the research report was done (at 2 AM the night before the deadline), he handled it with great pride, admiring especially his own drawings.

Bryan taught me the importance of handling and drawing the objects of his research. He liked describing what he knew visually. He liked touching the utensils. His research process demanded more than words. He also taught me something significant about topic choice. He needed to care about the topic he was researching. Although he raised some questions on his own, he was never truly invested in the study. If the teacher had allowed more choice within the broader scope of Colonial times, he might have found something he really cared about knowing in depth.

If I learned what *not* to do from one son's experiences, I learned what to do from his brother. Craig has loved the business world since he was little. I still have the note he wrote to the tooth fairy when he was only six years old: "I expect $1.00 or more or I want my tooth back." Or the note he left in his room before he fell asleep as we were getting ready for a yard sale before moving. "Dear Mom I do not want you to sell my tennis racket that Grampa gave me DO NOT SELL IT and I looked for stuff I don't need and so that you can sell it. I priced it already so you don't have to. I made sure that they were good prices. love Craig Good night"

When he was eleven, Craig started his first business. After school one day, he walked to the local university animal sciences department. He bought three chickens with his lunch money, tucked them into a paper bag, walked back to school and caught the late bus home. He wanted to earn money for himself. He had decided to raise chickens and sell the eggs. "How did you know which chickens to get?" I asked. "I asked the guy who runs the barn," he replied. He learned about other kinds of poultry by formulating questions, reading everything he could find on the topic, such as books written by people who raised poultry themselves, and asking experts at the university and kids he knew at school who belonged to 4-H.

By the time he was a senior in high school he had designed and built a barn filled with one hundred fifty laying hens, raised dozens of ducks and geese and showing hens, serviced several dozen egg customers, filled his room with ribbons and trophies from showing poultry at state fairs, and saved enough money to buy his first car. His ability to ask questions, questions that he wants answers to, and his ability to listen hard to answers, have been the cornerstones of his business expertise.

When I think about my own history as a "researcher" in our travel club, or my sons' experiences in and out of school, I realize that we must expand our notions of literacy to include all that we know and can do visually, physically, mathematically, and even sensually—through touch, taste, and sound. These ways of knowing our world enrich us as learners. My own experiences and my sons' have taught me that we learn the most when our research topic or issue matters deeply to us. When we have questions we want answered, we listen hard.

I want students to understand research as the process of engaging in a study that satisfies a deep curiosity, by learning:

- how to formulate their own questions
- where and how to collect information that answers those questions
- how to listen carefully
- how to explore a topic or issue in depth because it matters to them, and
- how to present information in a variety of unique ways

We must ask ourselves: When is the last time I really learned about something in depth? How did I go about learning it? How do I know I know this? Then our process of learning might change the way we approach research studies with our students.

Despite the fact I've just argued for free choice, there are times when we need to be pushed in directions we might not choose for ourselves. These directions give us a framework to our studies, yet allow us flexibility, as they push our thinking. I believe there are times when we need to establish parameters for our students. It pushes their thinking.

It's a curious phenomenon—when given too much freedom, many students don't know what to do with it. I wonder if that's because they still want and need the structure that specific guidelines provide. The majority of my seventh graders seem to work better within some parameters.

I don't think the topic or issue the students study is as important as teaching them the research process. Drawing boundaries makes the process more explicit.

But the *ways* in which I choose those parameters may be the reason the students can and do work so hard; they still find ways to care about what they are studying. I think of those topics, subjects, or issues that interest adolescents. I think of current events and issues that have substance. I think of the materials and persons that are available to the students, either directly from me in the classroom, in the school community, and/or within our town and state. And I try to set the parameters close to at least one other discipline so we can make connections.

I have found that asking seventh-grade students to consider endangered animals or environmental issues appeals to them for these reasons: They like animals; they care about environmental issues because they impact their world; they connect their language arts skills to applied science (pollution, acid rain, deforestation . . .) and social science issues; and what they learn pushes their thinking.

Still, no matter what boundaries I ask students to consider (environmental issues in seventh grade or human rights issues in eighth grade), I always tell them: "If you have a better idea for a topic and better ways of presenting your information, let's discuss them."

The structure of the research always begins the same way whether the students choose their own topics or I provide the limits of the research: What do you know? What do you want to know?

I provide the students with:

- choice (If they do not have free choice of any subject for research, I have to allow choices within the parameters. I never assign the exact topic.)

- time (I've found it takes a minimum of six weeks, and often eight to ten weeks to carry out thorough and thoughtful research.)

- response (Students receive positive, constructive responses to their work in progress and as final products through conferences and written comments.)

- organization (Students need written guidelines, organized strategies for collecting and saving information, available and easily accessible resources, schedules, and deadlines. They need long-range projects broken down into short-term chunks.)

- demonstrations (Students need to see examples of quality work from previous students and from the teacher. Before making an assignment, I try portions of it myself. If it isn't successful for me, it probably won't be successful for students.)

FRAMEWORK FOR RESEARCH

Background Information

Questions are the heart of research. But children often have difficulty coming up with questions because they don't know enough about the topic or issue. They need background information. If I'm giving students choices within a given topic, I read a picture book or passage from a novel out loud, or show a film or videotape that's rich with information about the general topic. I ask the students to listen to or watch for things that intrigue them and they want to know more about. They jot down those things in the notes section of their journals. Once they have begun to limit their choices, I show them what's available in my classroom for resources and take them to the library to read through encyclopedias or other resource books to gather some background information on their own. I want them to see what resources are available on their various choices. The students do not take notes, but they take an index card to jot down impressions and questions that come to mind as they read. From their initial informed impressions, they limit their choices further.

Formulating Questions

Questions give focus and direction to a research study, the same way a good lead does to a piece of writing. Researchers cannot gather information well unless they know what they're looking for while also staying open to surprise. I teach the students how to ask questions related to their topic.

Each student writes his or her topic on a large sheet of paper. I ask them to frame their questions around the old journalism heuristic: Who? What? Why? Where? When? and How? (I write down a topic of my own and list out my own questions.) After they go through a first round of questions—usually an odd number, seven to thirteen, that they really want answers to—I ask the students to leave their papers on their tables, stand, move to the student's paper to the right, read that student's topic and questions, and write a new question for the student researcher. We move around the room until the majority of students have written a new question on every student's paper. As students read their classmates' topics and questions, I tell them to do two things: Put checks next to the questions already asked that they would like to hear answers to, and write a new question that has not been asked.

Asking students to formulate questions for their peers performs multiple functions: It gives each researcher a variety of questions he or she might not have considered; it forces all students to read, write, and think as they examine the questions already asked and state unique ones of their own; and it helps each student researcher realize there's an audience for their findings.

This process also enriches the *search* of the research as students look for answers they might not have thought of on their own. It gives all students the opportunity to read many questions that influence their own research process. It teaches kids how to develop questions before serious reading begins.

Students read through these questions on their own sheets and star the twenty-one questions they believe to be the most urgent and fascinating to answer. The questions with the most checks guide their research. We brainstorm various categories their questions seem to fall into, such as, habitat, behaviors, communication, origins, migration, connections through literature (short stories, poems, legends, myths), unique characteristics, and enemies, if the majority of topics happen to be animals. The categories of questions differ depending on the parameters of the topics.

I show the students how to categorize their questions by color coding them with examples from my own research. If we are studying environmental issues I show them how they might use a red dot or check for all questions related to habitat, blue for questions related to enemies, and so on. We use 5 × 8 index cards, listing one category on the top of each card. After color coding, students transfer their questions to the respective cards. I even hole-punch the cards and clip or tie them together so kids won't lose them as they conduct their research.

I teach students how to cite their sources (books, people, videos, and so on) before the research even begins. They list all the references they use, as they use them, so they won't be scrambling to do so as the deadline approaches.

Searching for Answers

Depending on the topic, the student researcher may have first-hand knowledge from his or her own experience. They may use people, books, journal articles, videotapes, photographs, sketches, drawings, maps, charts, . . .any artifacts to reinforce and enhance their studies.

I want students to learn that often the best information comes from talking directly to experts in the field or to someone who has had first-hand experience with the topic or issue. Although I can't send students off-campus during the school day to interview people, when possible I bring experts to the classroom—a biologist who has been to the rainforest, a Shakespearean professor and his student actors, an animal-rights activist, a cartoonist, a writer, an animal researcher from the university, a Holocaust survivor. Bringing an expert into the classroom gives students an overview of the topic or issue, practice at asking questions and gathering information, and ideas from classmates and the guest that they may not have considered. I ask all students to have one or two questions prepared before the person arrives.

After the classroom visit, I ask students to write down questions they couldn't get answers to or those they'd like to explore further. They either set up an appointment to interview the person or send the questions to the person in a questionnaire format. (If they send a questionnaire, I show them how and why to include a self-addressed stamped envelope.) In preparation for an interview, they take notes on interviewing techniques, asking two or three big questions, formulating and asking follow-up questions, using or not using a tape recorder, and thanking the interviewee. Students may even videotape the person they interview.

I fill the classroom with books—fiction and nonfiction—magazines, posters, poetry; any resources related to their research subject. Using the categorized index cards, the search continues. I show students how to list facts and how to write down whole sentences that they find especially significant or particularly well worded based on the category on each card. I show them how to sketch and label. I reiterate the importance of citing sources. I also show them how to write down follow-up questions or personal thoughts that occur to them as they read, directly on the index card that they are using to record and sketch information.

After the information is gathered, I show students all the possible ways to present their findings, using the work of professionals and their peers. Those ways may include visual and oral possibilities. Sometimes the students have free choice; sometimes I ask them to try presenting information in prescribed ways.

Students are responsible for gathering information from a minimum of three different kinds of resources (experts, nonfiction books, films, firsthand observations, . . .) and they are responsible for presenting their findings in three different ways (informational pamphlets, editorials, picture books, song lyrics, fictional accounts, photographs, sketches, videotaped interviews, simulations. . .) Every finished product must include a process paper about how the product came to be and an evaluation of what was done well and what could have been done better, considering the process, the content, and mechanics of the product.

No matter what the research topic, I end with three questions to the students:

- What did you learn?
- If you had to conduct research again, on any topic, what's the process you would go through to do that?
- What could I have done differently to help you?

The two research projects that form the core of this book, *Rainforests: Drawing in All Disciplines*, and *Weaving the Threads of Response* were complicated, fun, successful, and immersed students in a wide range of ways for making meaning: reading, writing, speaking, listening, visual art, and music.

2 | RAIN FORESTS
Drawing in All Disciplines

I learned that . . . I don't want to tell my kids what a rain forest was; I want to show them what it is.

Amanda

I am watching David, one of my seventh graders, guide a five-year-old through our rain forest. She is gripping his hand tightly as her tiny feet shuffle their way through the hanging foliage of bushes and plants. Her eyes wander to the canopied ceiling past snakes wrapped around kapok trees and monkeys clinging to vines. The sounds of birds, falling water, heavy rain splattering against leaves, and distant thunder echo from every corner. She jumps as the roar of a panther surprises her. David tells her there is nothing to be afraid of, he'll take care of her. When she bends down and runs her tiny finger across the back of a paper-maché frog sitting on the edge of the pool that David and Jamie built—the one with running water—he smiles at me and whispers, "She thinks this is real. Isn't that awesome!"

Yes, David, this is awesome!

journal entry—L. Rief

Rain forests. I knew as much about them as my seventh grade students—next to nothing. That was one of the reasons we settled on the topic for our project. I wanted to teach the students how to conduct research, but I didn't want them to teach me things I already knew. I thought, too, that the rain forest was filled with vivid, lush sights and extraordinary sounds of the natural world—plants, animals, and people that held surprises for us. I knew, too, that this focus could be connected in so many ways to art and science. Most importantly, I believed learning about an ecosystem in danger would give us something to care about. It mattered. But how could it matter to these students who live so far away from any rain forest? I thought there would be a lot for all of us to learn.

THE SURPRISE OF RESEARCH

Good research should inform and surprise the writer as much as the reader. Questions formulated can lead to questions not yet considered.

And good research, like any good piece of writing, is usually for the writer first: the care put into it and the discoveries from it. In this particular case, I gave the students a parameter for research: rain forests. Within the topic, they made the research theirs by finding animals, plants, people, or issues about which they truly cared. Once they cared, they worked harder than I ever imagined they would, and learned more than I thought possible. If we think about the times your students have found the most success with *any* endeavor, and we'll find *caring* enveloping all they have done.

As the students conducted their research of the rain forest, I knew it would come to life for them if they could see it, touch it, and hear it. But we live in New Hampshire. A firsthand experience with a rain forest is not even a remote possibility. So we did the next best thing: We built one.

Originally three of us (Beth Doran Healey, an art teacher; John MacArthur, a sixth grade science and math teacher; and I) decided to work together to have our students engage in a project that would help them see the connections among our disciplines, that would appeal to many different learning styles, that would highlight the strengths and promises in the majority of students, that would be meaningful to them as learners by connecting to the real world, that would appeal to them emotionally, and that would still teach them all the basic skills of reading, writing, math, science, and art that formed the basis of each core curriculum.

We were standing in the hallway of the third floor of our building. No windows. Gray walls. Old radiators long since turned off. Dark. Dismal. And slated for long overdue renovations if the district residents would just pass a bond. I had just read Lynne Cherry's *The Great Kapok Tree*. "Let's build a rain forest!" I said. "Let's build it right here!"

We briefly sketched out what each of us would do. John MacArthur's math students would measure the walls and draw up architectural sketches. Their drawings and dimensions would be used by Beth Doran Healey's art students to design, construct, and paint the background (the sky, distant mountains, the very tops of the tallest trees), middle ground (overlapping trees and bushes on plywood panels with more detailed images of plants, flowers, and animals), and foreground areas (three-dimensional paper-mache plants, animals, and kapok trees) of the forest. My language-arts students would each choose a plant, animal, or people to study in depth by reading and writing in a variety of ways about all they found out. These same students would be in art classes to construct the figures based on the animal or plant they chose to study. In John's science class, students would study the plants, animals, and issues connected to rain forests that might impact us more locally along with other environmental issues.

So we constructed a rain forest in the third-floor hallway of our school. Alan Stuart, the industrial arts teacher, and Joan Savage from home economics, joined us in the project. Alan's students helped construct the huge three-dimensional kapok trees and Joan's students stitched sheets together to help form a canopy for the ceiling. And there were two of us in the language-arts classroom, as Maggie Moore was interning with me through the master's degree program at the University of New Hampshire.

We all learned how to work together, how to conduct research in any field and any subject, and how to use both writing and visuals as tools for realizing and solving some authentic problems. In addition, we all learned to be more aware of environmental issues by becoming more knowledgeable about the problems and the solutions. In the process, some students even learned how real research makes them reconsider their own futures.

THE RESEARCH PROCESS

Background Information

At the beginning of our project, the students knew little about rain forests other than having the vague notion that "they're being cut down and for some reason that's not good." They had no idea how the preservation of the rain forests was even remotely connected to them. I played an audiotape of tropical jungle sounds for background music as I read Lynne Cherry's *The Great Kapok Tree*. Not only are the animals appealing in this book, but the sounds of the rain forest are alluring. We all wanted to be there. The reading piqued their interest and the questions began: Why is the rain forest so important? Who is cutting it down? Why? How much of it has been destroyed? Where are the rain forests located? Which animals live there? What happens to them when the forest is destroyed? What can be done about it? These questions, along with others we added in the first few days, became the major questions for focused Group Visuals (Appendix A, Student Handout: Rainforest Research). When the questions come from the students they have a vested interest in the study. I'm part of the classroom also, and feel free to add some of my questions to the list for their consideration.

Rain forests seem so far away from us. It's hard for me to imagine how their destruction truly affects my life, or the lives of my students. The issues connected to the destruction of the rain forest are complex: economic; political; medical; aesthetic; environmental; . . . ethical. We tried to make sense of some of the complex issues surrounding the destruction of rain forests in the context of our responsibilities as individuals on this earth. I had enough copies of *The Rain Forest Book* (Lewis, 1990) for each student to read in class. While they followed along, I read the introduction, "Tropic of Concern," aloud. I reminded students that following along as someone reads actually helped them become much faster and more fluid readers. I told them to put checkmarks with pencils in the margins when I read anything that surprised them or they wanted to know more about. They were to put question marks in the margins next to any vocabulary words they did not completely understand. On an overhead transparency we summarized facts—such as, "1,500 species of birds—16 percent of all species of birds in the world—nest in the rain forests of Indonesia," listed and defined vocabulary, such as *endemic*, and listed questions that began to form in the students' minds, such as, "What can a single person in New Hampshire do to help preserve the rain forests?" So began our study of the rain forests.

Because there were only enough books for one class, we had to do our background reading in school. I divided the students into five groups of five to six students each. Each group was responsible for a chapter from *The Rain Forest Book*; they were to read it, take notes, and present their facts, questions, and vocabulary (words such as *epiphytes, ecosystem, biodiversity, canopy,* and *indigenous*) to the rest of the class. They had three days to read and prepare their presentations. My reading of the introduction served as their model.

Some groups had the best reader read aloud while the rest followed along. Some took turns reading pages aloud to each other. They all had to follow along and jot checks or question marks in the margins for later note taking and summarizing. I moved from group to group, simply nodding approval when the groups were working well, prodding, nudging, and suggesting when individuals needed help. During class presentations, all students took notes, including vocabulary words, from every other group.

We began, too, to notice words that inspired us. Margaret Mead's did. *"Never doubt that a small group of thoughtful, committed citizens can change the world. Indeed, it's the only thing that ever has."* (Lewis, 1990, p. 4) As did the words of Chief Seattle: *"The earth does not belong to us. We belong to the earth. . . . What befalls the earth befalls all the sons and daughters of the earth."* (Jeffers, 1991) We wrote the quotes on posterboard and hung them around the room.

Our discussion from Lewis's book gave direction to what we wanted to do: find a way to be that "small group of thoughtful, committed citizens" to change the world, if just a little. The students wanted to act on their findings. They wanted to save some of the rain forest. They believed that "building a rain forest" and writing about it would help others care also. I suggested informational pamphlets and picture books as two of the ways to teach others about specific plants and animals. The students suggested bookmarks to sell to raise money to "purchase" several acres. Eventually, students also suggested research questionnaires, so elementary children would know what to look for as they toured our rain forest; facepainting and puzzles or games, so they could leave with "a piece" of the forest; and reading of their own books and the stories of professionals, so listeners' interest would be piqued.

We watched the feature film *Medicine Man* for more background information about the research possibilities. We viewed the PBS video *Nature: Rain Forest (Selva Verde: The Green Jungle)* filled with the sights and sounds of the rain forest so students could select one animal or plant to study in depth. As we watched, I asked them to jot down at least seven different plants or animals that intrigued them and they wanted to know more about.

Once students chose a topic, we followed the research process for developing questions I described in "Keeping the *Search* in Research." Questions are vital to any research process. That doesn't mean we also shouldn't be open for surprises—those findings, bits of information that are unique and fascinating, and don't fit a category. In fact, we look for surprises.

To each collection of white, categorized index cards we added one colored card. On that card students jotted down the question they wanted to answer as part of the Group Visual. This way they could write down findings or sketch ideas as they were researching a particular plant or animal. One of the white cards was called "References," and I showed students the correct way to cite their sources as they worked.

I surrounded the students with books, fiction and nonfiction, poetry, journals, articles, and magazines such as *National Geographic*. They were always welcome to go to the school library if I didn't have enough resources available.

In addition to information and idea gathering from resources in the classroom, I expected students to read for a half hour each night from an extensive list of recommended books or reading they chose on their own that had something to do with animals or the natural world. Reading for a half hour each night and maintaining a "Reader's-Writer's Journal" is an ongoing expectation of mine, no matter what the focus of our reading or writing. They collect, react, respond, reflect in their journals, in words or pictures, with observations, descriptions, language, questions, and ideas.

I read aloud excerpts from several of these books to the students, to invite them in by showing them a flavor of the tone, language, and story from the recommended readings. I read this passage from *The Burning Season*, telling students this book was nonfiction, the true story about the murder of Chico Mendes and his fight for the rain forest:

> Visitors who stayed long enough to walk for a time in the surrounding forest discovered the bounty of the ecosystem that Mendes had died defending. It was a place of spectacular diversity and vitality. Turn over a log and find 50 species of beetle. Survey an acre and find 100 species of butterfly. In the Amazon, one type of rubber tree has exploding fruit that flings seeds 20 yards; three-toed sloths harbor dozens of species of insects and algae in their matted fur; river porpoises are cotton-candy pink. It was a living pharmacy that scientists had only just begun to explore. A fourth of all prescription drugs contain ingredients derived from tropical plants—malaria drugs and anesthetics and antibiotics and more—and less than 1 percent of the Amazon's plants had been studied.
>
> It became clear to outsiders that the murder was a microcosm of the larger crime: the unbridled destruction of the last great reservoir of biological diversity of Earth. Just a few centuries ago,

the planet had 15 million square miles of rain forest, an area five times that of the contiguous United States. Now three Americas' worth of forest were gone, with just 6.2 million square miles left. A third of the remaining rain forest was in the Amazon basin, and over the past decade alone, chain saws and fires had consumed about 10 percent of it—an area twice the size of California.

. . . In some ways, Chico Mendes and the rubber tappers were simply another endangered species, as much a part of the ecosystem as the trees they tapped, the birds in the branches, or the ants underfoot.

But the tappers were a species that was fighting back

(Revkin, 1990, pp. 15–16)

Students, therefore, had two different ways of responding to reading, in class and for homework: index cards that had been categorized with major questions for collecting factual information and anecdotes, and their journals for more thoughtful and thorough collecting and reacting in sketches or words to things they noticed. I pulled vocabulary words from passages I read aloud to students. From this passage, viewed on an overhead transparency so they could see it, I gave them the words *ecosystem, antibiotics, microcosm, contiguous,* and *aggression.* They copied parts of sentences surrounding each word, used the ellipsis to indicate missing words, and defined the words. I taught them how to break apart words by looking at prefixes and using the context of the sentence to decide which definition was correct. All of this went into the vocabulary section of their journal, with correct source citations. This way, students continued to learn language mechanics in context.

I told them, "Keep in mind all you'll be doing with this information: bookmark, pamphlet, picture book, controversial issue, group visual, and the building of a rain forest." I hung another quote that I love, from Romare Bearden, from the ceiling. "I think the artist has to be something like a whale, swimming with his mouth wide open, absorbing everything until he has what he really needs. When he finds that, he can start to make limitations. And then he really begins to grow." (Shange, 1994) "Read with your mouths wide open," I said.

I gave each of the students a handout (Appendix A, Student Handout: Rainforest Research) with an overview of the work expected and due dates for rough and final drafts. First rough-draft due dates help me work with the students as they move toward a final draft. They may go through many conferences with me, in which we talk about content before we edit that final, best draft. But I need at least those two dates—beginning and ending, so they are clear about the time frames within which they are working.

Students had ownership in the products as well as the processes, which I believe is one reason they worked so hard and so meticulously at all they did. These things mattered to them. They believed they mattered to others as well. They expected me to teach them how to make these products the best they could be.

THE PRODUCTS

Bookmarks

We decided bookmarks would be easy to sell—the perfect fundraiser for protecting as many acres of rain forest as possible. The more students found out about the plight of rain forests, the more they wanted to do something real to help. We sent the money earned to the World Wildlife Fund, which in turn sent specific information to the students about the acres of rain forest their money helped to protect. Out of more than fifty designs for bookmarks, students selected, and duplicated by hand, the ones they thought contained the most relevant "fast facts" and appealing illustrations that would cause the reader in turn to consider the worth of the rain forests.

Informational Pamphlets

Okapi. Living pine cone. New World monkey. Three-toed sloth. Margay. Kinkajou. Poison arrow frog. Agouti. Parakeet. Tree frog. Peccary. These are all animals from the rain forest about which there is little information. Seventh graders had to work hard to locate, gather, and organize their findings.

I believe pamphlets or brochures are the most sensible formats for students to use to disseminate factual information, instead of the usual ten-page report. We are handed pamphlets, brochures, or playbills everywhere we go: museums, zoos, theaters, doctors' offices, coffee shops, supermarkets, and so on. This is a format the real world uses to make vital information accessible quickly and accurately. Most of the students prepared their pamphlets by hand. Now the more technically astute students are teaching other students (and me) how to construct pamphlets on the computer.

Students used the categories that formed the basis of their research questions as the framework for the different sections of their pamphlets. Their categories and questions spread out on index cards gave them a strategy for gathering and sorting the information as they read, viewed, and listened to information. Instead of writing out in prose all they found, they worked on other ways to organize, analyze, integrate, and present their findings: poignant quotes, bulleted facts, labelled sketches, and so on.

These pamphlets were geared to a wider audience, particularly younger children, so the students knew they needed to make them colorful, inviting, and fun, as well as factual. Students drafted these pamphlets the same way they would any other piece of writing. We held conferences in which we discussed content first and mechanics last. I pointed out what they did well, raised questions for further investigation or modes of presentation, and made suggestions to help them make the pamphlets most effective

(Appendix B, Brian's Pamphlet: Macaw; Appendix C, Mike's Pamphlet: Jaguar).

To assess the final pamphlets, students created categories based on the criteria we developed to describe an effective pamphlet (Appendix D Evaluation of Research Pamphlet).

Walking students through this process of developing criteria guides the process as they work and gives them standards to meet. Teaching students how to assess their own work and the work of their peers helps them become more independent. They don't need me as the sole evaluator of all they do. I am teaching them how to recognize their strengths and how to improve on their weaknesses as they draft ideas.

Sarah's bookmark: front and back

Kevin's bookmark: front and back

Both were carefully drawn in bright magic marker with the lush, deep colors of the rain forest. Imagine the hot, bright orange of Kevin's sun, the deep green of the canopy, the snow white of the clouds, the blue of the sky—contrasted with the blazing sun on the otherwise empty back of his bookmark.

I love picture books—the rich, eloquent language, the lush artwork, the provocative, poignant ideas, and so often the deep, genuine emotion threaded through each book. *The Great Kapok Tree* has all of these elements, as does *Dear Children of the Earth*. I can barely make it through *Death of a Wombat* without crying when I read it out loud to students. I love *Here Is the Tropical Rainforest* for the close-up, detailed paintings, the cumulative effect of Dunphy's writing that shows how one thing affects another, and the fact that the author is an anthropologist who has studied the rain forest extensively and makes her findings accessible and meaningful to children. I adore *Stellaluna*, because it presents a bat from a totally unexpected point of view. And although I smile as I read *The Lorax* because of the language, or *Dear Mr. Blueberry* because of the wonderful imagination of the little girl, these stories still teach me plenty. These particular books are not specifically about the rain forest, but they illustrate to students how different authors use unique ways to convey their stories.

While the language and artwork of some picture books can challenge even the most proficient readers, the clarity and simplicity allow all readers access to fine books and complicated issues. Good picture books marry the finest language, poetic even in their prose, and art. I want students to have the opportunity to immerse themselves in the process of crafting language and complementing their ideas with pictures, or crafting pictures and complementing their illustrations with words.

"As secondary teachers," says Maureen Barbieri, "we need to know more about the power of the imagination, the mysteries of the creative process; we need to recapture the wonder of possibility. The artists remind us." (March 1993, 91) I agree with Barbieri, and I want the same thing for kids. Through picture books, children use their imaginations in ways to "recapture the wonder of possibilities." We don't invite these opportunities often enough. Pamphlets give students the opportunities to present factual information, but picture books invite them to use this information in conjunction with their imaginations. Recreate. Reinvent. Reimagine. Make this information yours. Make it so good it becomes ours.

For their picture book, Katie and Becky wrote and designed a pop-up book about many of the creatures that live in, on, or near the kapok tree. The text begins:

> "Farthest up you will see
> A green, immense canopy.
> This is where the top of me
> Meets the sky in harmony.
> I am the Kapok Tree! . . . One, two, three, four. . .
> How can there be so many more?
> Counting legs is so hard,
> So pull the tab and watch the centipede

Walkwalkwalkwalkwalk
Across the tunnel to a rock.
See the snake coiled so tight.
Oh how his colors s-s-s-seem so bright.
How does he sense what is on the tree?
Just pull the tab and you will s-s-s-see. . . ."

Brian wrote a picture book entitled *Fillers: And I Don't Mean Junk Food!*
He liked the way Eric Carle designed *The Grouchy Ladybug*, with each page
getting wider and wider as the grouchy ladybug encountered bigger and
bigger animals to antagonize. Brian designed an informational picture
book about recyclable objects. As the problems became bigger and bigger,
his pages became wider and wider: batteries to cans to styrofoam to paints
and oils to junk mail. His pages included a "Fast Fact" that would stun a
reader into acting, or at least reconsider his or her use of these non-
biodegradable items. He interviewed the manager of the Durham, NH,
landfill for facts and gathered the objects to draw.

Luke wrote and illustrated a moving-picture book, which can be pe-
rused on the accompanying CD, entitled, *Misha*, in which a tiger cub
awakens in her den:

Misha awoke, startled. There it was again! "Bang! Bang!" The
shots rang out. Misha whimpered uncomfortably into the dark,
earthy den, lonely and puzzled.

Misha, a three-month-old tiger cub just couldn't understand it.
What seemed just barely moments ago she had been nestled com-
fortably against her mother's stomach, dozing. Now, no one was
there.

Luke's lush watercolors truly enhance his text. In the story, Misha res-
cues his mother, and years later sees the poachers finally being led off by
"uniformed men."

No one worked harder than Jen, Sara, and Luke to create *Dear Mstr
Vktr*, a story through letters about a little girl who discovers a rain forest in
her closet and writes to a local scientist for advice on its care. The idea for
presenting the story through letters came from my reading of *Dear Mr.
Blueberry* by Simon James.

After hearing and seeing their first draft I knew they had a wonderful
story. They knew they needed to gather more information, especially about
how and what a first grader is able to write. Heather's letters had to sound
and look like a six-year-old's. They wanted Heather to be a "smart" first
grader. They set up an appointment to talk to a first grade teacher and to
look at some first grade samples of writing.

From that first grade teacher, Jennifer Hoginski, they learned that at
the beginning of the year children who can write, and want to write, often
put capital letters all along the left side of the page, whether it's the beginning of a sentence or not. They use periods sometimes, but seldom com-

mas. They capitalize names, and some *I* s, but usually only at the beginning of a sentence, not in the middle of a sentence. In this first-grade class Jennifer encouraged her students to keep a list of "wild words" that they had to spell correctly, such as *any, would, could, should, what, and when.* Jennifer corrected Sara's and Jen's drafts for wild words she would have given her students. Simple words, such as, *and, the, good, dear* were familiar to first graders. Sara and Jen revised accordingly, as Luke painted. The better the text became, the more Luke revised his paintings, as he wanted them to be the best he could do to correspond with their hard work on the story.

For both Sara and Jen, writing did not come easily. They worked hard developing the ideas. As their story idea began to coalesce, they worked as hard at invented, or temporary, spelling and getting the "mistakes"

Theres a Rainforest Growing
in my Closet
By Jen and Sara

Dear Barni,

My name is Heather. I'm a Kindrgardiner. My class is learing about the rainforest. Right now we're doing plants, sew my techer gave each of us a seed to grow at home. I put my seed in my pokit and forgot it was there. The next day when I opend my clawzit leaves were everyuere By the nextday there was a rainforest in my clawzit. My techer told us to take care of our plants, but I'm not sure how!

Right bak!,

Heather willims

Dear Heather,   ← good word!

I regret to tell you that rainforests can't grow in closatse. In order for them to grow they need sunsine and rain. I'm truly glad your class is studing the rainforeste. Maby you can do something to help it.

Your favorit ToVo friend,
Barni

Jen and Sara - This is fabulons! Wonderful idea!
Who is Barni? Why does Heather like his show
and why does she write to him about the rainforest?
Remember, 5 yr olds don't use many Vowels (a,e,i,o,u,
when they are learning to write.   ...y)
What could Barni suggest she does to help the RF?

Jen, Sara, and Luke's first draft of Dear Mstr Vktr.

right, as they did at getting Mr. Victor's language and syntax completely correct. They also had to embed factual information into the adult's letters, a wry sense of humor in both characters, vivid imagination in Heather's stubborn responses, and they had to keep the thread of a story going to hold the interest of readers, young and old. They even understood the possibility of sequel in their last line. Heather's postscript tells the reader that no matter what, Heather will not lose her imagination or the wonder of all possibilities. It made the story even more compelling to imagine the "ocean in her closet." No matter what the adult says, the child will not be deprived of her creations. Every reader loved the story—whether they were four or fifty-four.

Dear mr. vitre
mi Name is Heather
i'm in Grad One
I like wan you
came to arwre
class, i'm Irning
about the rane
forisste, we are
Doing Plense miy tichre Gave use
ech a Seed to Grow at home

I Poot min in my
pokit fgotit, the
naxst Day there was
a Rane foriste
in my Kozit.
my teaher told
us to take Kare
of owr Plans.
But I'm not
sher How.

what can I Do
to Keep the Plans
and anmols Holthy
rite Back

First grader's handwriting and spelling sample of Dear Mr. Vktr, written as Sara and Jen dictated their words to her.

Dear Mstr Vktr, or
The Rain Forest in my Closet
by Sara and Jen

Dear Mstr Vktr
Mi name is Heather im in grad one i likd wen you kam to ar klas
Im lrnin bout the ran forsits we ar doin plnc my techr gav us eech
A seed to grow at home I put myn in my pokit an fourgot it the
Nekst day ther was a ran forist in my closit my techr told us to
Tak kar of ar plnts but im not shur how wat can I do to keep the
Plnc an amenals hlthe
Rite bak Heather Williams

page 1

Dear Mr Viktr
I willent let any one stroi my ranforist. Its groen very big.
I opend the wndo so it gets sun and I waterd it.

  yor frnd alwas

     Heather

page 3

Dear Mstr. Viktr,
    I am protktin my ranforst but its groing to big. My shoos
slush when I walk and my best swetr is cot in the canapee and I
cant reech it and thers a flowr groing in my pokit. Its butiful red. I
need to do sumthin fast bekus leevs are sprowten and kuverin my
shus and the amanals are so lowd. The monkee howls all nite and
its hrd for me to sleep the frogs reebut and wake me up erly in the
mrning and ther are so many amanals I put a pillo ovr my hed
and tri to blok out the sonds but what should I do?

         your good frend

            Heather

page 5

Dear Mr Viktr,
    Aftr I got yor lettr befor I went to sleep I put the
bigges glas of watr in my closit and left my closit lite on
and left a penut butr sanwich for the anamals. Thank you
for yor vice.
         yor best frend

            Heather

page 7

Dear Heather,

    Thank you for your letter. I'm delighted to hear of your
concern for the rainforest, but I regret to tell you that rainforests
can't grow in closets. In order for them to grow they need
sunshine and lots of rain.
    I'm truly glad your class is studying rainforests. They
provide us with oxygen, food, and medicines. Rainforests cover
more than two percent of the earth's surface and are home to
more than fifty percent of the earth's plants and animals. But the
rainforests are being destroyed fast; people take the trees for
wood and clear the land for farming by burning down
thousands of acres. Did you know that once a rainforest is
destroyed, it can't grow back?
    Maybe you can help the rainforest.

         Truly yours,

            Mr. Victor

page 2

Dear Heather,

    I'm glad your rainforest is better. It needs lots of sunshine
and water. But it can't live in a closet! The canopy reaches
almost 250 feet into the sky. So you see, a rainforest is much too
big for a closet.

         I'm sorry,

            Mr. Victor

P. S. Maybe you could contribute something to the rainforest so it
stays protected.

Dear Heather,

    As much as you don't want to believe this, a rainforest
cannot grow in a person's closet, and animals can't live in a
closed space! They need food, water, air, and sun. They can't
get that while living in a closet. It's good you can use your
imagination but, I must repeat, rainforests do not grow in closets.
    But, that doesn't mean you have to stop caring for the
rainforest. It still needs all the help it can get.

         Sincerely,

            Mr. Victor

page 6

Dear Heather,

    I admire your tenacity through sleepless nights for taking
all the right steps to help preserve the rainforest you imagine is
in your closet. You are right to give it light, food, and water.
    Unfortunately, other people are burning the rainforest for
land and other purposes, such as using the wood to make
furniture, or as firewood. Also, the trees are home to many
animals. Animals like the Poison Arrow Frog and Emerald Tree
Boa are losing their homes.
    But what these people don't realize, or don't care about, is
that once the rainforest is destroyed it can't grow back. We all
lose the unique plants like the bromeliad and the passion fruit.
Have you ever tasted a passion fruit? Did you know there's an
animal called the Living Pinecone?

         Sincerely,

            Mr. Victor

page 8

Dear mr Viktr

If you visitd me you could see the molde sloth climing a kapok tree. Hes funny he climes sooo slo. Bring a umbrela. The rainforist is leeking into my room. I promis I wont dstroy this one. But aftr I red your lettr I toled all the aminals thay cant liv in a closd up plas but they didint leev until the fire strtd. I think sum bad men came last nite and burnt my rainforist. I calld 911 on my fishr pric foen. No anser. Am I gonna be urestd for stroyin my rainforist.

alwas your best frend
Heather

page 9

Dear Mr. Viktor

I tuk your vice and my mom calld the nachur convrtore and when I woke up the nekst day my rainforist was gone. It was bettr if it livd sumwer els like brasl or kostarika with the othr rainforists. It was dark and skare in my closit.

your bestest frend

Heather

PS My techer gave me a seeshel. I can hear the oshun in it. I put it in my closit.

Final version of Dear Mstr Vktr, page 11.

Dear Heather,

Although there is not a rainforest growing in your closet, destroying the rainforest is serious!

Did you know that rainforests twice the size of Florida are wiped out each year? Maybe you can call or write to someone to help save the other rainforests.

Good luck,

Mr. Victor

P.S. No, Heather, you will not be arrested for destroying the rainforest in your closet. You have tried really hard to preserve it.

page 10

I surround the students with picture books. I read books aloud, and examine the text, noticing especially metaphorical language, incorporation of information, sense of details, leads, endings, use of repetition, the range of characters and what each wanted, and the point of the story. We consider the format of the picture books; were they letters? series of poems? narrative? rebus? ABC? We look just as carefully at pictures. What did colors, shapes, and size show us? How do the illustrations complement or enhance the text? What difference does layout on the page make? What surprises do we notice?

We can't just surround our students with books. The experience will be richer and more meaningful if we also showcase a few books, demonstrating what to look for, and teaching our students about the delightful subtle complexities of picture books. We looked carefully, for example, at Jon Scieszka's and Lane Smith's *The True Story of the Three Little Pigs*. Students noticed the wolf's bow tie, his glasses, and his handkerchief covered with pictures of pink, fluffy sheep. The subtlety of the pictures, as well as the wolf's rational words, implied that he was truly a sweet, misunderstood wolf. With guidance students realize that authors and illustrators make intentional choices that lead readers to certain conclusions.

Controversial Issues

Although I wanted students to write about controversial topics connected to the rain forest—environmental interests versus economic realities, ani-

21

mal testing, farming and deforestation—so they could really begin to understand the two sides to each issue, we never had the time. We spent a full three months on our range of topics, and simply ran out of time.

A few students did manage to draft several ideas regarding controversial topics. Jeanne and Larisa interviewed several experts about the pros and cons of animal testing and drafted a story that incorporated both sides of all they learned. Here's the lead to their second draft:

> Maggie watched grimly as her mother applied her makeup. The tons of tiny bottles, cans, and tubes were making her sick. How many animals had died? she wondered. She could barely watch her mom dab, smear, brush, and glide all those things onto her face.
>
> She plopped down on the couch and flicked on the TV. Her mind was working furiously. Ever since they had done that animal testing project in school she had been so concerned. She did all that she could to get her mom to switch to makeup from natural products.
>
> *Her mother almost drove her mad, but nothing worked. Maggie was running out of ideas.*
>
> *Her mother walked out of the bedroom with a really nice dress on. Maggie would have commented on it, but the makeup stopped her. Her mom took out her fur coat. Maggie flinched as if someone had slapped her. . . .*

Conor and Sam wrote to Ben and Jerry (of ice cream fame).

> Dear Ben and Jerry,
>
> We're in the seventh grade and we're doing a rain forest project. We're building a rain forest out of all recycled materials. We are going to be selling Rainforest Crunch ice cream and other rain forest products. The money we make from selling them will go to an undecided conservation fund for the rain forest.
>
> We were wondering if you could donate some of your product, Rainforest Crunch ice cream, or could you let us buy at wholesale or discount price? We could get the ice cream from a store you deliver to in Durham, NH, like Classic Cone or Durham Marketplace.
>
> The rain forest has taken 240 million years to evolve and we could destroy it in sixty years. The rain forest belongs to history and the natives and the animals. We have no right to destroy it. And once it's destroyed, it's gone for good.
>
> The rain forest covers 2 percent of the earth's surface and it contains 50 percent of the earth's animals. We depend on the rain forest for many things, including air, medicines, humidity, and temperature control. We may even DIE if the rain forest is destroyed. If the rain forest is destroyed:

- The earth will warm up, the polar ice caps will melt, and the earth will perish in water.
- The roots of the rain forest hold much of the earth together, so if the rain forest is destroyed, the earth might fall apart.
- We will die from loss of oxygen.
- All of your ice cream will melt.

With your donation we can make sure a portion of the rain forest is not destroyed. Please think about what we said, and either write or call back. Thank you for your consideration.

Next time, no matter what the focus of our study, I would make sure there is time to consider the controversial issues related to the students' topics. Our democracy is founded on multiple perspectives, differing opinions, and even, at times, contentious dissent. It is so important that we teach our students to see the various sides of issues through informed research, informed discussion, and informed decision making. We live, work, and play in communities through the art of compromise. How do the actions of one person or group impact others? In what ways does that matter? These are the questions our students must consider. We need to provide the time and encouragement.

Group Visuals and Curricula Guides

Both the group visuals and the curricula guides originated with the students. Through the Group Visuals, students wanted to clarify further all they had learned about specific areas related to the ecosystem. Visuals made those focused areas clearer. In the same way that questions helped them clarify their own research, questions would help the elementary students focus on and investigate more carefully particular areas of our rain forest.

As they constructed their visuals, students referred back to notes and sketches they had collected on their colored cards. Students with the same question met in groups, drafted and sketched ideas, and met in conferences with Maggie Moore, my intern, or me, before final drafting the answers to their questions on posters.

Research questionnaires are much like curricula guides. Each small group of four to five students requested a grade level—kindergarten through fifth grade—and constructed a set of questions to guide the younger children as they toured our rain forest and our classrooms. It was so interesting to listen in on seventh graders as they tried to decide how well elementary students could read and understand and care about all they were asking. They came to the conclusion that the guide/questionnaire for the younger students had to be much simpler than the guide for the older students. We decided to combine several of the guides, pulling the best questions and ideas from each student group, to form a questionnaire. Seventh graders used their expertise as older sisters and brothers to construct these guides (Appendix E, Research Questionnaire: Kindergarten to Grade 3; Appendix F, Research Questionnaire: Grades 4–5).

As soon as John MacArthur's sixth-grade science students realized the seventh graders were writing curricula guides in the form of research questionnaires, they wanted to design something that students could take with them to do after they left our rain forest to keep the memory of the forest alive for them. They designed games and puzzles, which rose in degree of difficulty based on the grade levels of the students. (Please see accompanying CD.)

EVALUATION

I want kids to become evaluators of their own work. When they are responsible for developing the criteria on which they must evaluate themselves, they take the entire process more seriously and hold themselves, and their classmates, accountable for all they believe should have been done—and should have been done well. We have to teach kids how to develop criteria for an effective piece of writing. In the case of the informational pamphlets, we looked at numerous pamphlets from previous years as well as those professionally developed and distributed in various fields, from health classes to museums, in order to identify the elements impor-

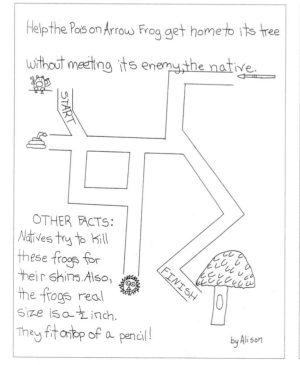

Rain forest maze for first and second graders.

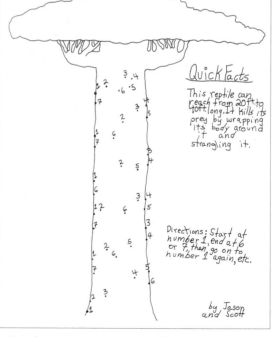

Rain forest connect-the-dots for third and fourth graders.

tant to the pamphlet (Appendix D, Evaluation of Research Pamphlet).
From these evaluations, students selected the best pamphlets to post for
younger students to read as they toured our rain forest. Students composed the research questionnaire for fourth and fifth graders (Appendix F,
Research Questionnaire: Grades 4 and 5) to answer because, in the sev-
enth-graders' words, "They'll only read the pamphlets if we give them a
reason to read them." (When we go on field trips now, I make sure to give
the students a "reason" to look carefully at certain exhibitions or sites.)

As part of the evaluation of their picture-book project, I asked students to complete a case history of their book (Appendix G, Process Paper:
Evaluation of Picture Book), how it came to be from initial inception to the
final design of both the text and the illustrations.

Whole-class instruction included how to:

- gather questions before conducting research
- write follow-up questions
- take notes, including use of "shorthand"
- find and track information in a text (* or ? in margins, on sticky notes, tabs)
- use a table of contents, chapter headings, and an index
- read for information
- conduct an interview
- write references for resources used
- find, note, and return to vocabulary (? in margins, on sticky notes, tabs)
- define words in context
- define words using prefixes and roots
- write a pamphlet or brochure
- write a picture book
- write a business letter
- write an opinion piece or essay
- revise for content (based on type of writing: pointing out what was included and done well, questioning what was missing or needed clari-
  fication, suggesting what needed to be added)
- edit for directions to a reader (the how, what, and why)
  indenting; bulleting information; capitalizing of proper names, titles,
  headings, beginnings of sentences; different usage of *there, their, they're,
  its, it's, affect, effect*; use of quotation marks for dialogue or short pieces of
  writing; and the use of an ellipsis, period, exclamation mark, question
  mark, comma, colon, semicolon, hyphen, dash, apostrophe.
- write an evaluation
- write an analysis

This list is by no means complete. Examining the students' projects
and the processes they went through to get there (their rough drafts),
shows me clearly what they know and can do, how they have grown, and
what they've learned. Students are graded in the areas of process (good
faith participation as evidenced in their rough drafts and daily attention to

tasks at hand), the content (based on the criteria we develop together for the kind of writing product they are creating), and mechanics (how well they executed the directions—periods signal a stop, quotation marks signal a speaker, and so forth—for a reader).

But it's their big questions that matter most. What did their research mean to the community? What did constructing a rain forest mean to them? What did they learn from this project? Their answers to these questions mattered far more than if they had said, "I learned how to use an ellipsis."

RESPONSE

Community Response

We put out pens and note paper on clip boards so visitors could respond to our rain forest as they left.

> This is fabulous! What a lot of hard work, dedication, imagination, and artistry. This is the kind of energy that will save the rain forest!
>
> Great job! Good to see so much concern about the environment—it will be your generation's greatest problem and opportunity.
>
> (from a parent)

> WOW! You people did a grate job   (Mark 5 years old)

> At first I really didn't think much about the rain forest or have much interest in it. I didn't even know how badly it was really in trouble. But after we worked on it, if I see a paper on it, I read it. If there is a show about it on TV, I'll watch it. I realize how important the rain forest is to everyone and why we need it so badly. How many cures for sickness are in there? How many insects, plants, trees, flowers, animals, and fruits that we use . . . or will use some day?
>
> Alyssa

> I learned how helpful it is to work together. If our whole class didn't help we wouldn't have had a rain forest. I learned how we need the rain forest, what's happening to it, and what we can do to help. How to tell younger kids about it so they would understand. I learned what animals, medicines, and plants thrive in the rain forest. I learned so much it's hard to say it all but I learned more than I have about any subject.
>
> Ben

> I went to the Museum of Science in Boston. On the Omnimax I saw rain forest life and destruction. In the end I noticed one per-

son crying. . . . (Through my research) I learned how incredibly important the rain forest is for all the species. . . . I learned that if everyone works together we can accomplish the impossible. . . . It was everyone contributing together to make the rain forest what it was. And in a sadder way it is everyone contributing to the destruction of the rain forest. That is what I believe is the message that this generation should get. **We can do it.** We can stop the destruction of the rain forest through communication and writing, as I did in the newsletter. . . . Now I understand why that woman was crying in the Omnimax Theater.

Larisa

AFTERTHOUGHTS

We built a rain forest several years ago (Appendix O, Guide to the Rain Forest). We have not conducted the same study since. What matters is that we now know our students and what interests them. We now know our communities and what affects them. No matter what focus our research takes, we try to center ourselves and our students in studies that:

- connect the disciplines in natural ways
- appeal to and reinforce many different learning styles
- highlight the strengths and promises in the majority of students
- are sensible to the students as learners because the study matters in the real world
- appeal to students academically, practically, aesthetically, and emotionally
- teach them the skills of our disciplines in the context of the study
- encourage investigation of the students' own questions for vested interest

When all these factors can be put into place, we might be able to teach our students to care in the same way *Birdfoot's Grampa* (Caduto and Bruchac, *Keepers of the Earth*, 1988) does:

> The old man
> must have stopped our car
> two dozen times to climb out
> and gather into his hands
> the small toads blinded
> by our lights and leaping,
> live drops of rain.
>
> The rain was falling,
> a mist about his white hair
> and I kept saying
> you can't save them all,
> accept it, get back in
> we've got places to go.

But, leathery hands full
of wet brown life,
knee deep in the summer
roadside grass,
he just smiled and said
*they have places to go
too.*

—Joseph Bruchac
Entering Onondaga

REFERENCES

Works Cited

BARBIERI, MAUREEN. March 1993. "Listen for the Ringing: Benedict and Carlisle's *Beyond Words." English Journal*, NCTE, Vol.82, No.3.

CANNON, JANELL. 1993. *Stellaluna*. Orlando, FL: Harcourt Brace and Company.

CARLE, ERIC. 1977. *The Grouchy Ladybug*. New York: Thomas Y. Crowell.

CHERRY, LYNNE. 1990. *The Great Kapok Tree*. San Diego, CA: Gulliver Books.

DUNPHY, MADELEINE. 1994. *Here Is the Tropical Rain Forest*. New York: Hyperion.

JAMES, SIMON. 1991. *Dear Mr. Blueberry*. New York: Margaret K. McElderry Books.

JEFFERS, SUSAN. 1991. *Brother Eagle, Sister Sky*. NY: Dial Books.

LEWIS, SCOTT. 1990. *The Rainforest Book: How You Can Save the World's Rain forests*. Los Angeles, CA: Living Planet Press.

Medicine Man. Producer Andrew J. Vagna.

Nature: Rain Forest (Selva Verde: The Green Jungle). 1985. Dir. Phil Agland. Public Broadcasting Service.

REVKIN, ANDREW. 1990. *The Burning Season*. New York: A Plume Book.

SCIESZKA, JON and LANE SMITH. 1989. *The True Story of the Three Little Pigs*. New York: Viking Kestrel.

SHANGE, NTOZAKE. 1994. *I live in music*. New York: Stewart, Tabori & Chang.

SCHIMMEL, SCHIM. 1994. *Dear Children of the Earth: A Letter from Home*. Minocqua, WI: NorthWord Press.

SMITH, IVAN. 1976. *The Death of a Wombat*. Melbourne, Australia: Sun Books.

World Wildlife Fund: 90 Eglinton Ave. E., Suite 504, Toronto, Ontario M4P 2Z7 Canada.

Additional Rain Forest References

Picture Books

CHERRY, LYNNE. 1990. *The Great Kapok Tree*. San Diego, CA: Gulliver Books.

CHERRY, LYNNE. 1998. *The Shaman's Apprentice*. San Diego, CA: Gulliver Books.

COWCHER, HELEN. 1988. *Rainforest*. London: Andre Deautsch Limited.

DORROS, ARTHUR. 1990. *Rain Forest Secrets*. New York: Scholastic.

DUNPHY, MADELEINE. 1994. *Here Is the Tropical Rain Forest*. New York: Hyperion.

HAMILTON, VIRGINIA. 1995. *Jaguarundi*. New York: The Blue Sky Press.

JORDAN, MARTIN and TANIS. 1991. *Journey of the Red-Eyed Tree Frog*. New York: Green Tiger Press.

JORDAN, MARTIN and TANIS. 1993. *Jungle Days Jungle Nights*. New York: Kingfisher Books.

LEWIN, TED. 1993. *Amazon Boy*. New York: Macmillan.

National Geographic Action Book: *Explore a Tropical Forest*.

PRATT, KRISTIN JOY. 1992. *A Walk in the Rainforest*. Nevada City, CA: DAWN.

RYDER, JOANNE. 1996. *Jaguar in the Rain Forest*. New York: Morrow Junior Books.
YOLEN, JANE. 1993. *Welcome to the Green House*. New York: Putnam.

Informational

BAKER, LUCY. 1990. *Life in the Rain forests*. New York: Scholastic.
CHERRY, LYNNE (Ed.). Nov./Dec. 1993. "Tropical Rain Forests". *Nature's Course*. Vol.2, No.2.
CORNELL, JOSEPH. 1979. *Sharing Nature with Children*. Nevada City, CA: Dawn Publ.
GALLANT, ROY A. 1991. *Earth's Vanishing Forests*. New York: Macmillan.
GEORGE, JEAN CRAIGHEAD. 1990. *One Day in the Tropical Rain Forest*. New York: HarperCollins.
GEORGE, MICHAEL. 1993. *Rain Forest*. Mankato, MN: Creative Editions.
GREENAWAY, THERESA. 1994. *Jungle*. New York: Alfred A. Knopf.
HARE, TONY. 1990. *Rainforest Destruction*. New York: Watts.
HIRSCHI, RON. 1993. *Save Our Forests*. New York: Delacorte Press.
JAVNA, JOHN. 1990. *50 Simple Things Kids Can Do to Save the Earth*. New York: The Earth
    Works Group.
LESSEM, DON. 1995. *Inside the Amazing Amazon*. New York: Crown.
LEVINE, SUSAN A. 1990. *Save Our Planet: 52 Easy Things Kids Can Do Now*. New York: Para-
    chute Press.
LEWINGTON, ANNA. 1993. *Antonio's Rain Forest*. Minneapolis, MN: Carolrhoda Books.
LEWIS, SCOTT. 1990. *The Rainforest Book: How You Can Save The World's Rain forests*. Los Ange-
    les, CA: Living Planet Press.
    This book has an especially comprehensive listing of resources available for further in-
formation and study.
OPPENHEIM, JOANNE. 1994. *Floratorium*. New York: Bantam.
REVKIN, ANDREW. 1990. *The Burning Season*. New York: Penguin Books.
SILCOCK, LISA (Ed.). 1990. *The Rain forests: A Celebration*. San Francisco: Chronicle Books.
TAYLOR, BARBARA and FRANK GREENWAY. 1992. *Rain Forest: A Close-up Look at the Natural World
    of a Rain Forest*. New York: Dorling Kindersley.
Voyages of Discovery. 1993. *Trees and Forests*. New York: Scholastic.

Audiotape

KRAUSE, BERNIE. 1989. *Environmental Sounds: Tropical Jungle*. Berkeley, CA: The Nature Company.

Videotape

DUDLEY MOORE (Narrator). 1994. *Totally Tropical Rain Forest*. National Geographic Society.

Environmental Issues in General

Collections

CADUTO, MICHAEL J. and JOSEPH BRUCHAC. 1991. *Keepers of the Animals: Native American Stories
    and Wildlife Activities for Children*. Golden, CO: Fulcrum Publ.
CADUTO, MICHAEL J. and JOSEPH BRUCHAC. 1988. *Keepers of the Earth: Native American Stories
    and Environmental Activities for Children*. Golden, CO: Fulcrum Publ.
ELKINGTON, JOHN. 1990. *Going Green: A Kid's Handbook to Saving the Planet*. New York: Puffin.
EXLEY, RICHARD and HELEN (Ed.). 1985. *My World Nature: Thoughts and Illustrations from the
    Children of all Nations*. Lincolnwood, IL: Passport Books.
FACKLAM, MARGERY. 1990. *And Then There Was One: The Mysteries of Extinction*. CA: Sierra Club
    Books.
FEW, ROGER. 1993. *Children's Guide to Endangered Animals*. New York: Macmillan.
FIELD, NANCY and SALLY MACHLIS. 1990. *Discovering Endangered Species: A Nature Activity Book*.
    Middleton, WI: Dog-Eared Publications.
POLLOCK, STEVE. 1993. *The Atlas of Endangered Animals*. New York: Facts on File, Inc.
PRINGLE, LAURENCE. 1991. *Living Treasure: Saving Earth's Threatened Biodiversity*. New York:
    William Morrow.

Articles/Periodicals

CHADWICK, DOUGLAS H. March 1995. "Dead or Alive: The Endangered Species Act." *National Geographic*. Vol.187, No.3.

Nature's Course, Ed. Lynne Cherry. The Center for Children's Environmental Literature, P.O. Box 5995, Washington, DC 20016

A quarterly newsletter with a different environmental focus in each issue. Excellent information.

The Children's Rain Forest, P.O. Box 936, Lewiston, ME 04240

Publishes an Educational Resources Guide for a minimal amount, containing lists of teacher's guides, audiovisual materials, and newsletters on the rain forest.

Read Alouds

These are unique presentational formats and illustrations to show to students for ideas:

CARLE, ERIC. 1977. *The Grouchy Ladybug*. New York: Thomas Y. Crowell.

The unique way of presenting facts and the method of making the pages bigger and bigger, as the animals the ladybug encounters get bigger and bigger, is an interesting format to show students.

CHERRY, LYNNE. 1990. *The Great Kapok Tree*. San Diego, CA: Gulliver Books.

With the music of the rain forest playing in the background, this is an inviting introduction to the study of the rain forest.

CHERRY, LYNNE. 1997. *Flute's Journey: The Life of a Wood Thrush*. New York: A Gulliver Green Book.

CHERRY, LYNNE. 1995. *The Dragon and the Unicorn*. New York: A Gulliver Green Book.

DUNPHY, MADELEINE. 1994. *Here Is the Tropical Rain Forest*. New York: Hyperion.

FLEMING, DENISE. 1996. *Where Once There Was Wood*. New York: Henry Holt.

GREELEY, VALERIE. 1990. *White is the Moon*. New York: Macmillan Publ.

The repetition and predictability make this a good book for students to view as a unique way of shaping a book for young children.

GEISEL, THEODOR SEUSS. 1971. *The Lorax*. New York: Random House.

JAMES, SIMON. 1991. *Dear Mr. Blueberry*. New York: Margaret K. McElderry Books.

JEFFERS, SUSAN. 1991. *Brother Eagle, Sister Sky*. New York: Dial Books.

JEWETT, SARAH ORNE. 1990 (Illustrations by Douglas Alvord). *A White Heron* (first published in 1886 by Houghton Mifflin Co). Gardner, ME: Tilbury House.

LASKY, KATHRYN. 1995. *She's Wearing a Dead Bird on Her Head!* New York: Hyperion.

PALLOTTA, JERRY. 1993. *The Extinct Alphabet Book*. Watertown, MA: Charlesbridge Publ.

SCHIMMEL, SCHIM. 1994. *Dear Children of the Earth: A letter from home*. Minocqua, WI: North-Word Press.

Poetry

COLE, WILLIAM. 1978. *An Arkful of Animals*. Boston: Houghton Mifflin.

KUMIN, MAXINE. 1989. *Nurture*. New York: Penquin Books.

NICHOLLS, JUDITH (Ed.). 1989. *What on Earth. . . ? Poems with a Conservation Theme*. Boston: faber and faber.

SULLIVAN, CHARLES (Ed.). 1996. *Imaginary Animals*. New York: Harry N. Abrams.

WOOD, NANCY. 1995. *Dancing Moons*. New York: Delacorte Press.

WOOD, NANCY. 1993. *Spirit Walker*. New York: Delacorte Press.

WOOD, NANCY. 1974. *Many Winters*. New York: Doubleday.

YOLEN, JANE. 1986. *Ring of Earth*. New York: Harcourt Brace Jovanovich.

YOLEN, JANE. 1996. *Mother Earth Father Sky: Poems of Our Planet*. Honesdale, PA: Boyds Mills Press.

Chapter Books

CARSON, RACHEL. 1964. *Silent Spring*. New York: Houghton Mifflin.

GEORGE, JEAN CRAIGHEAD. 1983. *The Talking Earth*. New York: HarperTrophy.

GEORGE, JEAN CRAIGHEAD. 1992. *The Missing `Gator of Gumbo Limbo*. New York: HarperTrophy.

GEORGE, JEAN CRAIGHEAD. 1992. *Who Really Killed Cock Robin?* New York: HarperTrophy.

GEORGE, JEAN CRAIGHEAD. 1972. *Julie of the Wolves*. New York: HarperTrophy.

GEORGE, JEAN CRAIGHEAD. 1989. *Water Sky*. New York: HarperTrophy.

HOBBS, WILL. 1988. *Changes in Latitudes*. New York: Atheneum.

KLASS, DAVID. 1994. *California Blue*. New York: Scholastic.

LASKY, KATHRYN. 1988. *Home Free*. New York: Dell.

MIKAELSEN, BEN. 1995. *Stranded*. New York: Hyperion.

MIKAELSEN, BEN. 1991. *Rescue Josh McGuire*. New York: Hyperion.

REVKIN, ANDREW. 1990. *The Burning Season*. New York: A Plume Book.

RYLANT, CYNTHIA. 1985. *Every Living Thing*. New York: Aladdin.

SHARPE, SUSAN. 1990. *Waterman's Boy*. New York: Bradbury.

WEINBERG, LARRY. 1984. *The Cry of the Seals*. New York: Bantam.

Sketching, Illustrating, Art

ARNOSKY, JIM. 1983. *Secrets of a Wildlife Watcher*. New York: Lothrop, Lee and Shepard Books.

ARNOSKY, JIM. 1982. *Drawing from Nature*. New York: Lothrop, Lee and Shepard Books.

BERRY, JAMES. 1996. *Rough Sketch: Beginning*. Orlando, FL: Harcourt Brace and Company.

BOICE, JUDITH (Ed.). 1992. *Mother Earth Through the Eyes of Women Photographers and Writers*. San Francisco, CA: Sierra Club Books.

CARLE, ERIC. 1996. *The Art of Eric Carle*. New York: Philomel Books.

CARLE, ERIC. 1993. *Eric Carle: Picture Writer* (videotape). New York: Philomel Books.

CHANCER, JONI and GINA RESTER-ZODROW. 1997. *Moon Journals: Writing, Art, and Inquiry Through Focused Nature Study*. Portsmouth, NH: Heinemann.

CHANCER, JONI and GINA RESTER-ZODROW. "Sketches of Life". *Voices From the Middle*. Eds Barbieri and Rief. NCTE. Vol.4, No.3, September 1997.

COLLINS, PAT LOWERY. 1992. *I Am an Artist*. Brookfield, CT: The Millbrook Press.

CUMMINGS, PAT (Ed.). 1992. *Talking with Artists*. New York: Bradbury Press.

CUMMINGS, PAT (Ed.). 1995. *Talking with Artists*, Vol.2. New York: Simon and Schuster.

ERNST, KAREN. 1994. *Picturing Learning: Artists and Writers in the Classroom*. Portsmouth, NH: Heinemann.

GAYLORD, SUSAN KAPUSCINSKI. 1994. *Multicultural Books to Make and Share*. New York: Scholastic.

HARDEN, ELISABETH. 1995. *Print Making*. Edison, NJ: Chartwell Books.

JOHNSON, CATHY. 1992. *Creating Textures in Watercolor*. Cincinnati, OH: North Light Books.

JOHNSON, CATHY. 1995. *Painting Watercolors*. Cincinnati, OH: North Light Books.

LOCKER, THOMAS. 1995. *Sky Tree* (Seeing Science Through Art). New York: HarperCollins.

O'BRIEN, MARGARET and URSULA SHEPHERD. 1990. *Nature Notes: a Notebook Companion to the Seasons*. Golden, CO: Fulcrum Publ.

ROOP, PETER and CONNIE. 1993. *Capturing Nature: The Writings and Art of John James Audubon*. New York: Walker and Company.

WRIGHT-FRIERSON, VIRGINIA. 1995. *A Desert Scrapbook: Dawn to Dusk in the Sonoran Desert*. New York: Simon and Schuster.

PICTURING POSSIBILITIES

*We need to work toward making our classrooms workshops of
learning—a literate community filled with opportunities for
many ways of making meaning, surrounded with the works of
artists, scientists, writers, and mathematicians, so that
students can participate in apprenticeships of learning. As
students begin to express themselves in many modes, it will be
through our close observation that we can learn how they
make connections with a work of art, a piece of literature, a
poem, a song, or a dance. We need to observe our classrooms
from outside and inside, to make our students our curricular
informants.*   (Ernst, 1994, p.166)

By watching my students and collecting their work over the years, I've
learned how vision and voice matter to them. Their reader's–writer's journals are filled with sketches, drawings, and photographs; they are filled
with poems and song lyrics. Their portfolios are heavy with best-loved or
most-difficult musical pieces, family pictures, bar and bat mitzvah
speeches, church sermons, audiotaped poems, play performances, and art
work from science and social-studies classes. Students make sense of
themselves and their worlds through more than words, as do I. My journals and portfolio are filled with sketches, and pictures—old family photos, pictures of students at work, pictures of people and places that matter
to me—that help me tell the story of who I am as a literate human being. I
encourage the students to show me all the ways they can tell their stories
of who they are as literate young men and women.

We can't build a "rain forest" every year, nor do we have the resources
to pull together such a massive project each year. But there are things I can
do daily on a small scale in my language arts classes to encourage students
to include the visual arts in their learning lives. We live in color. We live in
pictures. As a teacher I'd like to see what my students see and understand.
I'd like them to see what I see and understand. I'd like to see how their pictures and words connect and help them make sense of their lives.

Students keep reader's–writer's journals. I tell them: "As you read,
write, and live in the world, collect what you think, hear, see, observe,
wonder, believe, discover, feel, question, notice, realize, imagine. As a human being, what do you care about? Your sketches and drawings matter as
much as your words."

I ask students to write down the words of Walker Evans, a photogra-
pher, on the first page of their journals: "Stare. It is the way to educate your

eye and more. Stare, pry, listen, eavesdrop. Die knowing something. You are not here long." (*Voices from the Middle*, Sept.97, p.45)

In the same way, I show students examples of sketches and journal entries from previous students, and how they came about. I show them several examples of my sketches and drawings, and some from professional writers and artists. I also teach them one or two simple techniques for sketching that I learned from Karen Ernst, Joni Chancer, and Gina Rester-Zodrow. Using leaves and shells, we all make several contour drawings just to learn to look closely at something. I point out where all the materials and books are for writing, drawing, paper-cuts, and painting. Then, I invite them to join the process. Unless otherwise noted, all of the examples included here were written or drawn in the students' journals. They are the seeds of their ideas for future, more polished pieces.

THROUGH JOURNAL SKETCHES

The Classroom

I ask students to find and draw the object in the room that matters the most to them as readers and writers. I have drawing paper and No.2 pencils available, as pens and lined journal pages are not easy to draw on. In their journals I ask them to answer the questions: "What did you choose to draw? How is that important to you as a reader and writer? What did you learn about yourself as an artist or about drawing?"

For my own journal sketch, as I searched the room for what was most important to me, I realized it was the students. I tried to capture them reading, writing, drawing, and getting comfortable in the room. It took time and a lot of erasing to get these sketches "right." At the time I had no idea what I would do with the drawings, other than capture what I valued most. Later, however, I realized that I wanted to use these sketches on a pamphlet for parents informing them about my philosophy and goals for the language-arts program and recommending books and authors to them. Parents frequently ask: "What can we expect? Can you recommend books and authors to us for our sons and daughters?" I show the students the pamphlet. I want them to see I am using my writing and sketching for real reasons for real audiences.

Field Trip Observations

Whether we are going outdoors to a particular site (pond, playing field, nature path), to a play, or to a museum; whether the trip is for my class or another class, I ask students to bring their journals and find one thing to sketch. On a field trip to the Boston Aquarium for science, we had 110 students spread throughout the building, carefully sketching, labeling, and writing after the tour.

Kaitlin chose to sketch and write about jellyfish. She may do nothing

I'm proud of these pictures. I feel like I captured a lot of what I value - kids writing, reading, getting comfortable with the room, materials...
I realized I capture more of what I see if I take my time and really look at it. (I need to give kids that Moffett poem - To Look at Anything) I learned again that I can't do everything. I don't have the time to concentrate heavily on drawing + illustrating but I do want to value pictures as a way of communicating thoughts, ideas, and feelings. (Same w/ drama)

"Exactly how do you teach writing to eighth graders," the woman on my right asked, continuing the polite conversation at this community fund raiser. "Slowly," I laughed. "One student at a time."

Jessi writes!

What did you choose to draw?
How is that important to you as a R-W in this class?
What did you learn @ yourself as an artist, or about drawing?
What have I learned: that without kids this room doesn't matter to me
- that my journal is the place where I store every-thing that makes me think, wonder, figure out, remember...

Caitlin

I like these sketches, too, because they look like the kids in real life. I know it's Jessi + Caitlin. Brad's head is not this small, but the rest is right. And I like that I captured the perspective of his legs - and shoes!

Three girls were sitting at the table by the window. Savitri limped across the room, smiled, put her book bag down, and took the 4th seat. One girl rolled her eyes - all 3 stood + moved to another table...

Brad

Sept. 23rd

Rief journal entry on September 23.

Language Arts

In the language arts I want students to emerge from the classroom with the ability to:

* enjoy writing, reading, speaking, and listening
* use language effectively to create knowledge, make meaning, challenge thinking, and build community in their lives
* reflect on, and evaluate their own language use
* recognize and evaluate the ways in which others use language to affect them
* value their own language, and accept and appreciate the language of others
* know how to learn in any field with the lifelong appreciation of language arts skills
* as independent learners, making and trusting their own choices

My **standing homework assignment** for each student is to:

* read for a half hour each night

* collect/respond/react/reflect daily in his/her reader's- writer's journal
(3-5 pages per week)

* maintain a reading list of books read

* find and define 3-5 vocabulary words in context per week

* keep a spelling list of frequently misspelled words

Each student will bring his or her portfolio and reader's-writer's journal home at the end of each quarter.

Team Concept

As an adolescent, the middle school student is searching for appropriate roles and directions in life. Through a team concept (four academic teachers working with the same students throughout the year) our major goal is to afford numerous opportunities for all of our students to express thoughts, to challenge ideas, and to weigh values.

We believe that students become informed, clear thinking citizens by participating actively in all of our classes as readers, writers, viewers, speakers, and listeners.

Our goal is to teach our students how to develop into articulate, literate young men and women, who:
* believe learning is for life
* become independent learners
* contribute creatively and productively in our society
* communicate effectively with others
* understand the world in which they live
* find their place in this complex, diverse world
* know their differences are their strengths

Parents are the first, and most important, teachers in their children's lives. Thank you for your continual support.

"...if I want my children to develop an indestructible sense of wonder, then I must first develop my own."
Katherine Paterson, Gates of Excellence

Language Arts
Information for Parents and Students
ORMS
1998-99

Linda Rief

Jessi writes!

Caitlin

"The hardest battle is to be nobody but yourself in a world that is doing its best, night and day, to make you like everybody else." ee cummings

---

What Good Readers Do

* read for pleasure
* re-read a loved book again and again
* read the same author
* read a variety of materials, including nonfiction, picture books, poetry, magazines, popular fiction, young adult books, newspapers,...
* abandon books
* use context clues to guess meanings of words
* trust book recommendations from friends
* look for comfortable spots to read

In class your son or daughter will choose books to read on his or her own; we will read poetry, essays, picture books, short stories, novels, and plays together as a whole class; we will read recommended titles in small groups; and we will read aloud to each other daily.

You can surround your son or daughter with reading materials that interest him or her. Show them you value reading by reading yourself. Read aloud to your daughter or son and invite her or him to read aloud to you.

Brad

Recommended Reading and Authors

Angelou: I Know Why the Caged Bird Sings
Armstrong: Sounder
Avi: The Confessions of Charlotte Doyle
Card: Ender's Game
Cheripko: Imitate the Tiger
Cisneros: House on Mango Street
Cormier: The Chocolate War; Tunes for Bears to Dance To
Courtenay: The Power of One
Creech: Walk Two Moons; Chasing Redbird
Crutcher: Ironman; Stotan!; Athletic Shorts; Staying Fat for Sarah Byrnes; Running Loose
Cushman: Catherine Called Birdy; The Midwife's Apprentice
Dorris: Sees Behind Trees; The Window
Draper: Tears of a Tiger
Gibbons: Ellen Foster
Giff: Lily's Crossing
Hayden: One Child; Somebody Else's Kids
Hesse: Out of the Dust; Letters from Rifka; Phoenix Rising
Hinton: The Outsiders
Hobbs: Downriver; Beardance; Bearstone
Kay: Phantom
Levine: Ella Enchanted
Mazer: When She Was Good
McCammon: Boy's Life
MacLachlan: Journey
Paterson: The Great Gilly Hopkins; Lyddie
Paulsen: Woodsong; The Car; Brian's Song; Father Water, Mother Woods; Nightjohn; Hatchet
Philbrick: Freak the Mighty
Pullman: The Golden Compass
Rawlings: The Yearling
Rawls: Where the Red Fern Grows
Rylant: But I'll Be Back Again; A Couple of Kooks; Missing May; The Van Gogh Cafe
Steinbeck: Of Mice and Men
Townsend: The Secret Diary of Adrian Mole
Voigt: Dicey's Song; The Runner
Wolff: Make Lemonade
Woodson: From the Notebooks of Melanin Sun
Wynne-Jones: The Maestro
Yolen: The Devil's Arithmetic, White Jenna

These authors have many other titles that are equally good. This list includes books with difficult issues, as well as challenging language.

Readers' Reflections

When I read a good book my brain does backflips. Suddenly there are new possibilities to be explored-- new ideas. Suddenly, I have questions, thoughts.
Emma

I'm reading a mouthwatering book.... Just listen to this. A woman once asked John Viehman, "Why walk?" and he said, "Because the world looks different at two miles an hour? Because spring comes one flower at a time? Because a mountain reveals itself to those who climb it? Because I like the drama of crags and gullies emerging from behind a curtain of mist?..."
Seth

Read like a wolf eats. Gary Paulsen

I finished this book (One Child) standing in the bathroom, and cried. My mom, who had been passing by, asked if I was okay and spoiled the moment. Kaitlin

A literate person, in the broadest sense of the word, is one who is continually reading, writing, thinking, listening, and evaluating for real purposes in real-life situations.
Regie Routman Transitions

I learned that the freedom to choose and the time to read are not luxuries... They are the well-spring of student literacy and literary appreciation. Nancie Atwell In the Middle

Language-arts pamphlet

Kaitlin's journal entry

9/19
Responses to the Aquarium trip
Observations of Jellyfish:

Their bell-shaped heads like a bubble
blown by a child,
So perfect and delicuite, strands of
Angel hair sweep gently—
in a current like a wind in late summer
Reflections play upon the lumniscent
bells from glowing blue lights,
And the Jellyfish dance,
bathed in their dim light above and
below them,
for they have no boundaries, no limits.
They repeat their movement, and I
know not why.
But why reason out something
glorious, if bewilderness is part of its
beauty.

*Kaitlin, did you write this? It's beautiful.
Your words move like the jellyfish — they
sweep gently across the page.*

with this entry other than capture the moment, but her sketch and words hold the potential for a piece of poetry. In science class, she may decide to study jellyfish more in depth, and this may become part of her study incorporated into a children's picture book, an informational pamphlet, or a variety of other choices.

Response to Literature—Whole-class Reading

Using a piece of literature that brings visually rich images to mind, I ask all the students to write down the passages that really make them see, think, and feel something. I ask them to sketch what they see. (I make sure that drawing paper, colored pencils, and thin magic markers are available at every table.) I ask students to write out what the passages and sketch bring to mind.

In this particular case, we read the story "Eleven" by Sandra Cisneros. I had enough copies so that all students could read along as I read aloud. I asked two students, who are fluent, animated readers, to read the parts of

"This is when I wish I wasn't eleven, because all the years inside of me—ten, nine, eight, seven, six, five, four, three, two, one—are pushing at the back of my eyes. When I put one arm through one sleeve of the sweater, which, smells like cottage cheese and then the other arm through the other and just stood there with my arms apart as if the sweater hurts me and it does, all ichy and full of germs that aren't even mine."

"I wish I was anything but eleven because I want today to be far away already, far away like a runaway balloon, like a tiny o in the sky, so tiny-tiny you have to close your eyes to see it."

"Eleven"

I drew this because it would be awful to have to wear something that isn't yours. And as embarrassing as that would already be, crying would make it even worse. I think that the red balloon represented the girl in a way because she probably would have wanted to drift off into nowhere. I can imagine and feel this sweater. Once in 3rd grade my teacher yelled from across the room for me to go get a boy named Matt to read to our class. But I thought she said, "a mat." So I went to Matt's class and brought back a pile of rugs/mats. Matt was sitting in the rocking chair reading and everyone froze. I immediately realized what was going on and dropped the rugs crying. It was awful, but what made it worse was when I came home. The teacher, who I got the rugs from, was there (because she was my mom's friend and she told my mom laughing. It was really embarrassing.

Kirsten's sketch and journal entry

*Brian's sketch and journal
entry*

**October 2
Brian's response to
"Eleven" by Sandra Cisneros**

I wouldn't put on that sweater. There
might be germs in it or lice. I would
leave if she tried to make me put it on.
It would make me so mad. I've known
teachers like Mrs. Price and maybe they
should get another kind of job. She
wouldn't listen to what the girl was saying. I hate it when teachers won't listen
to you. It makes me so mad.

Mrs. Price

Mrs. Price and Rachel. I highlighted their parts in yellow so there was no
fumbling as we read.

We talk about stories like this and the readers' responses. We look at
all the different reactions. Students need to see that we all react differently
to reading, and yet we draw some common understandings from the text
to support our thinking.

Observations Outside of School

I show students how I sketch those things that I love, that matter to me, or
that fascinate me—things I don't want to forget. Sometimes I don't know
what I'll do later with these pictures or words, I just know I want to capture them.

I was waiting for a plane at the airport in Anchorage, Alaska, when I
spotted an incredible exhibit of baskets and masks. I fell in love with one
large, coiled basket and started to sketch it. It was nearly impossible to capture the weave. I read a poem next to the baskets, a poem that touched me
deeply because I kept thinking, this is why I love baskets and quilts. When I
touch them I feel the "presence of my ancestors." It is in our roots that we discover who we are. It is in my writing and sketching that I am trying to discover who I am.

I wrote down the poem by April Varnell Davis. Some day I will use her
words to inspire my own words. And I sketched the mask. I had no colored
pencils with me so I had to label colors. I discovered in the sketching that
the harder I looked at the mask, the more detail I saw. As I tried to capture
this carved piece of art, I not only understood how much work the carving
was, but I began to have an appreciation and understanding of its essence.

As I drew I understood more clearly why I wanted kids to draw. In the
beginning of the year Caitlin made a list.

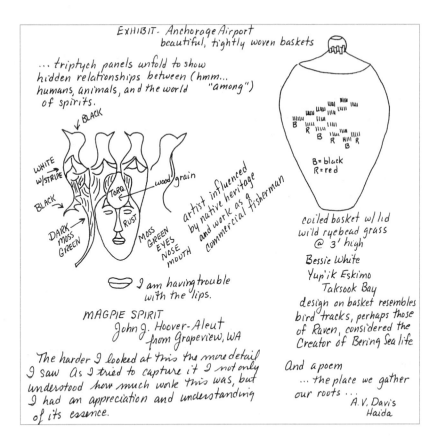

*Reif's journal entry and
sketches*

Seven things more important to me than school

- enjoying life
- being a good person: as a friend, as a daughter, as a sister
- learning about stuff that interests me: birds, plants, ancient cultures, animals
- gardening
- being kind to everything
- running
- basketball

So many of the things that she really cares about show up in her journal as sketches and comments. These sketches and journal entries were first-draft thinkings that led to more polished pieces of writing. It all started with sketching those things she cared deeply about.

The more I look at Caitlin's sketches, her written responses, and her poetry, I think she is writing as much about herself as she is about the world around her that she observes so closely and cares about so deeply. She is gaining an appreciation and understanding of the world in which she lives. I am gaining an understanding and appreciation for Caitlin, because I am truly seeing who she is through her drawing and writing.

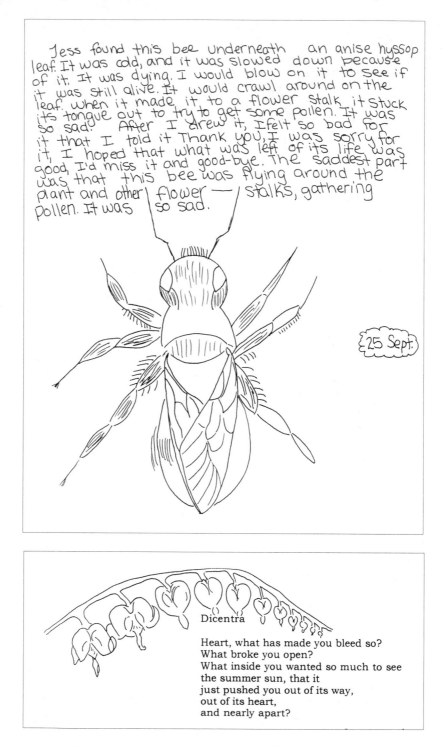

Jess found this bee underneath an anise hyssop leaf. It was cold, and it was slowed down because of it. It was dying. I would blow on it to see if it was still alive. It would crawl around on the leaf. When it made it to a flower stalk it stuck its tongue out to try to get some pollen. It was so sad. After I drew it, I felt so bad for it that I told it Thank you, I was sorry for it, I hoped that what was left of its life was good, I'd miss it and good-bye. The saddest part was that this bee was flying around the plant and other flower — stalks, gathering pollen. It was so sad.

25 Sept.

Dicentra

Heart, what has made you bleed so?
What broke you open?
What inside you wanted so much to see
the summer sun, that it
just pushed you out of its way,
out of its heart,
and nearly apart?

I learn about Molly in the same way. She wonders who she is, where she fits, how hard it is being thirteen. She writes:

> I hate being 13. I hate being not quite an adult, but not a child either. They should have a test to determine your maturity (like, if you got a low score you have to go back to 3rd grade, and if you get a really high score, you go straight to graduate school.)

Molly, too, takes some of this first-draft thinking and crafts a poem called "Patent Leather Agony." "Who am I? Where do I fit?" she asks in these sketches and writings. I hear Molly's voice.

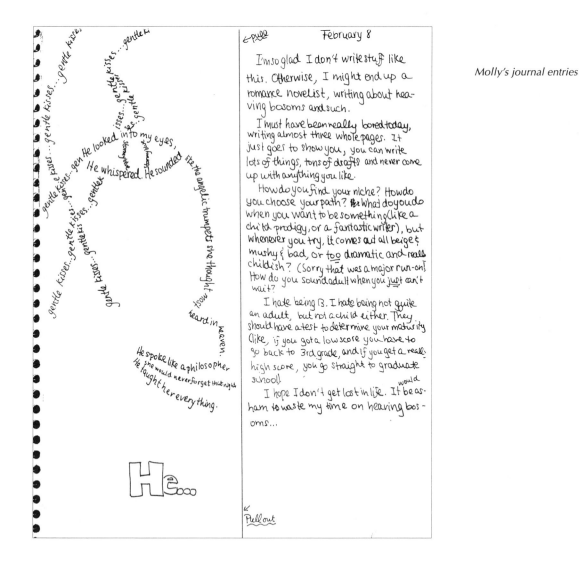

Molly's journal entries

Molly's journal entries (Continued)

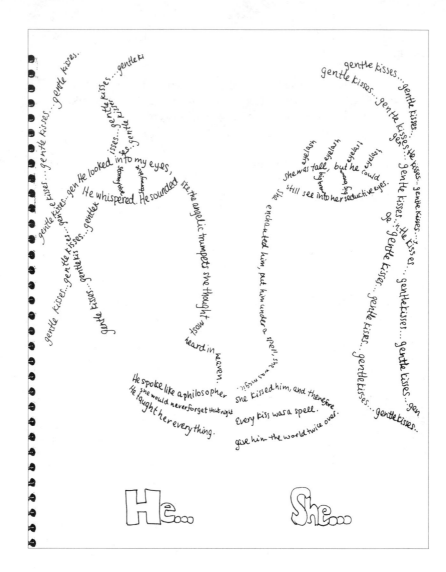

Response to Reading—Individual Choice

Students are asked to read for a half hour each night—anything of their own choice. In response to that reading, they must fill three to five pages in their journal. They may write and sketch.

Silas sketches fishing flies he has tied to illustrate new techniques he is learning as he reads fly-tying books and attends classes. He colors and labels each one. He writes out the history behind the names of these elaborate hooks. He shows me the equipment he uses, the plastic boxes of flies carefully stored, and the books from which he is learning. He is astounded and ecstatic that he is allowed to read these nonfiction books he

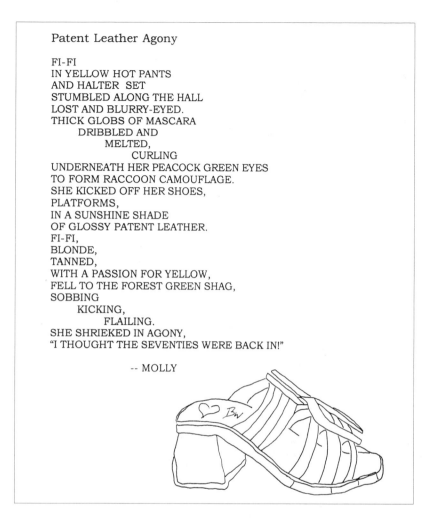

Patent Leather Agony

FI-FI
IN YELLOW HOT PANTS
AND HALTER SET
STUMBLED ALONG THE HALL
LOST AND BLURRY-EYED.
THICK GLOBS OF MASCARA
         DRIBBLED AND
                 MELTED,
                         CURLING
UNDERNEATH HER PEACOCK GREEN EYES
TO FORM RACCOON CAMOUFLAGE.
SHE KICKED OFF HER SHOES,
PLATFORMS,
IN A SUNSHINE SHADE
OF GLOSSY PATENT LEATHER.
FI-FI,
BLONDE,
TANNED,
WITH A PASSION FOR YELLOW,
FELL TO THE FOREST GREEN SHAG,
SOBBING
        KICKING,
                FLAILING.
SHE SHRIEKED IN AGONY,
"I THOUGHT THE SEVENTIES WERE BACK IN!"

                    -- MOLLY

Molly's Poem Patent Leather Agony

loves—for school! Silas even has me write a note in his journal to show his dad, explaining why he is indeed encouraged to read and discuss these books of his own choice. (I assure his dad we are reading "literature" in class.)

Pam sketches from the covers and pages of the books she picks up. She thinks a lot about the drawings even if she isn't deeply invested in the words. The more she draws, the more she is pulled into the reading. She becomes more thoughtful. By the time she gets to *Shabanu*, the more she cares about the characters.

When Pam finishes reading *Shabanu* she decides she wants to take one of her sketches to final draft. She *sees* the desert and the importance of these camels to the main character. Her drawing will be one of her final drafts for the six-week period.

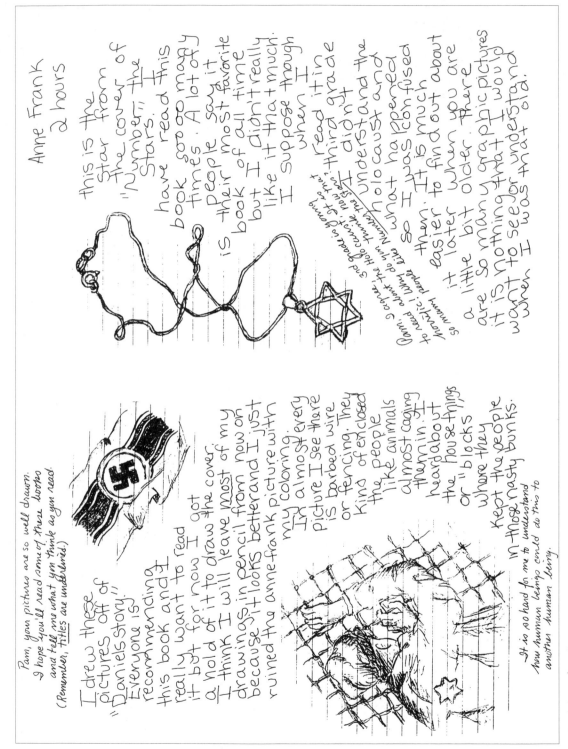

Pam, your pictures are so well drawn. I hope you'll read some of these books and tell me what you think as you read. (Remember, titles are underlined.)

I drew these pictures off of "Daniels Story." Everyone is recommending this book and I really want to read it but for now I got a hold of it to draw the cover. I think I will leave most of my drawings in pencil from now on because it looks better and I just ruined the anne frank picture with my coloring. In almost every picture I see there is barbed wire or fencing. They kind of enclosed the people like animals almost caging them in. It was hard about the house things or "blocks" where they kept the people in those nasty bunks.

It is so hard for me to understand how human beings could do this to another human being.

Anne Frank
2 hours

this is the star from the cover of "Number the Stars." I have read this book so so many times. A lot of people say it is their most favorite book of all time but I didn't really like it that much. I suppose though when I read it in third grade I didn't understand the holocaust and what happened then. It is much easier to find out about it later when you are a little bit older. There are so many graphic pictures it is nothing that I would want to see or understand when I was that old.

Pam, I want you to read it and give it a chance. It might be different. I think you will like it. (so much!!!)

Pam's journal entries.

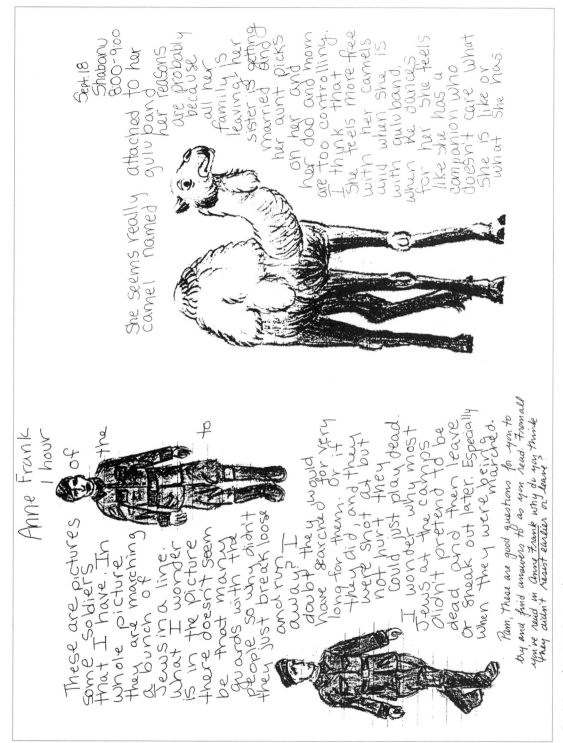

Anne Frank
1 hour

These are pictures of some soldiers that I have. In the whole picture they are marching a bunch of Jews in a line. What I wonder is in the picture there doesn't seem to be that many guards with the people so why didn't they just break loose and run away? I doubt they would have searched for very long for them. Or if they did, and then were shot at but not hurt they could just play dead. I wonder why most Jews at the camps didn't pretend to be dead and then leave or sneak out later. Especially when they were being marched.

Pam, these are good questions for you to try and find answers to as you read. From all you've read in Anne Frank why do you think they didn't resist earlier or leave?

Sept.18
Shabanu
8:00-9:00

She seems really camel named attached to her guluband her reasons are probably because all her family is leaving her. her sister is getting married and her aunt picks on her and her dad and mom are too controlling. I think that. She feels more free with her camels and when she is with guluband. when she dances for her she feels like she has a companion who doesn't care what she is like or what she has.

Pam's journal entries (Continued).

Kirsten's journal was filled with finely detailed drawings of flowers and leaves. One day I heard her talking about trying to earn some money. I suggested she use these drawings to make up notecards, five to a pack, to sell at the school store. She is now investigating the cost of copying, heavy note paper, and wrapping.

Nicole's journal was filled with stylistic sketches of her peers. I suggested that she make bookmarks. She is now investigating costs of color copying and laminating.

Kids want to *do* things with their ideas. If we can help them see the possibilities, it helps them value their own strengths.

Kirsten's note cards.   *Nicole's bookmark.*

Loves and Hates Chart

I ask students to make a list of loves and hates in their journals. From that list they draw an illustrated, graduated chart of loves and hates, being as specific as possible. From these illustrated charts I ask them to take one or two things and tell me more about each.

Like Katie, many students list friends and family at the top of their lists of loves. From these lists, and conferences with the students in which they tell me more about various things, students find and draft pieces of writing. Sometimes the words come before the illustrations; other times the illustrations come before the words.

Jeff, who struggled with writing and wasn't terribly confident with words, found an idea as he wrote "Jen" and illustrated exactly what he meant.

Kirsten's family topped her list of loves. Her journal was filled with

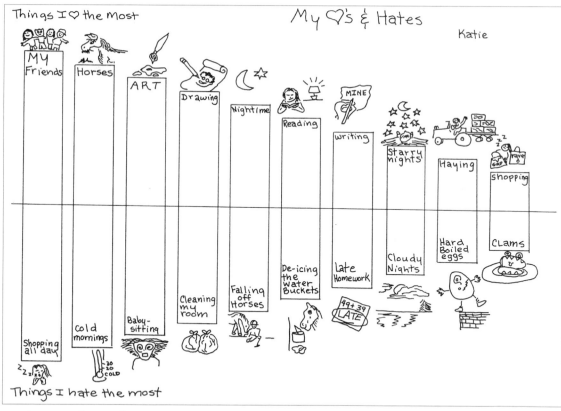

Katie's Loves and Hates chart.

JEN

I asked you to dance,
but you were still crying.
I gave you a rose,
but you were still depressed.
I gave you a teddy bear,
but you never received it.
I gave you a porcelain unicorn,
but you were still broken up.
I tried to be nice,
I tried to comfort you,
I tried to help you,
but none of it worked.
So I cried.
And you don't know
how much it would mean to me,
just to see you,

   smile.

Jeff

Jeff's Jen *with illustrations.*

sketches of her little sister and older sister. It was no surprise that her writing too turned to family, and focused nostalgically on loss—the loss of the way her family was before her parents divorced—in her piece, "Days at the Farmhouse."

Providing kids with an occasional framework for an idea gives them ideas they might not think of on their own. When they tell me they have nothing to write about we can refer back to this chart and talk about each item.

Days at the Farmhouse
by Kirsten

When I was a little girl living in my family's farmhouse, we had many pets. The goats and sheep stayed in the barn, while the cats and dogs lived in the house. I used to walk to the barn down the long, curvy dirt driveway in the back of our house. I held onto my mother's soft, strong hand, with my dad and my sisters trailing behind as we walked. I inhaled the warm, spring air as we reached the field where the goats and sheep were grazing.

My younger sister squealed whenever a sheep licked her salty fingers. My mom, stilled holding my hand, helped me pick a bouquest of dandelions and clovers. My dad carried handfuls of hay as he walked through the bright green grass toward the goats. With his big, dark fingers, he fed their hungry mouths. He used to pick up my small body, up and over the pointy fence to pet the sheep.

Spring in the field changed to popsicles dripping down my salty fingers in the sweltering heat of the summer sun. With my yellow jump rope I skipped down to the barn and whipped rocks into the humid air. I used to stop at the well to fill a bucket of water for the hot, sweaty animals. As I was pouring the icy, cool water into their dirty dishes, they lapped it up with their rough tongues.

In September the fields turned to piles of newly raked red and yellow leaves. With pieces of grass and leaves stuck in our hair from jumping in piles of leaves, my sister and I tumbled our way down to the barn. We both stepped up onto the wooden stools to look into the pen of goats. As my outstretched hand smoothed their rough curls, I noticed that their wool coats were quickly growing back.

Now it is December. Leaves give way to white, frosty windows. I walk down the short, not so curvy dirt driveway. Alone. My dull brown boots, covered in muddy slush are buried under snow. When I reach the barn my pink fingers wrap slowly around the metal handle and I step into the barn. It doesn't smell like hay anymore and there is no sound except my breath escaping into the cold air. It numbs my nose. Everything is gone. The goats and sheep have been given away, the family has left, and I am too old to be picked up.

Kirsten's sketch of Sister and Days at the Farmhouse

I draw for myself. I do not draw to teach or educate.

—Charles Schultz

Every day before Latin class began at Oyster River High School in Durham, NH, Lincoln (a student) drew a cartoon on the blackboard. Every day, the teacher walked into class and erased his cartoon.

I flinched when Lincoln Peirce, now, a syndicated cartoonist with his *Big Nate* comic strip, told this story on a visit to my classroom several years ago. How many times had I told my seventh and eighth graders not to doodle in their journals, even the kids whose drawings I actually admired? How many times had I told them to stop drawing on the white board? What made me think this kind of writing didn't count? After all, I adore *Peanuts*. Charles Schultz had to start somewhere, as well.

Peirce was visiting the classroom after I read in the newspaper that his daily comic strip, *Big Nate*, was about to go into national syndication. I had also read that Peirce had drawn his first cartoons while a student at Oyster River Middle School—our school. I wanted Peirce to show my students, and me, that cartoons weren't useless doodles. Kids seem to love cartoons, even the serious ones like *Maus*. When I took the time to ask the students, they explained the complex thinking they went through to create a cartoon. They knew what they were doing, cared about what they were doing, and I had been dismissing all their efforts. I didn't know enough about cartooning.

Big Nate, syndicated by United Features Syndicates, is about a sixth-grade boy who thinks he's a great artist and doodles while he should be doing his homework. It also features Nate's fifteen-year-old sister, his father, an unpleasant social-studies teacher, and a friend named Francis. Much of Peirce's inspiration comes from his own childhood and his experiences as a former teacher. He didn't think any cartoonists were writing or drawing about school. Because sixth grade was a significant year for *firsts*—first dance, first art class, first romantic thoughts about girls—he placed Nate in sixth grade. Several years ago, he retrieved all his middle school notebooks from his parents' attic to use for ideas.

"To be a good cartoonist," Peirce said to our class, "you must be first and foremost a good writer. You're more likely to create a good comic strip if you're a good writer and bad artist, than you are if you're a bad writer and a good artist."

Peirce suggested that aspiring cartoonists start by copying other cartoonists they admire until they gain confidence in their own abilities. "It helped me to learn how to draw," he said, referring to his copying of *Peanuts* cartoons and *Calvin and Hobbes* over and over again when he was a child. "These are cartooning at its best," he said. "Great writing and great drawing. . . . Then I wanted to make characters of my own." From Lincoln Peirce we learned:

- cartoonists are writers
- to use our own life experiences for story
- that cartoons are about people—best characters are ourselves, family, and friends
- how to take a round, expressionless face and give it emotion
- cartooning shorthand to give directions or information to a reader, and feelings to a character
- dialogue (in balloons), sound effects (symbols), and captions (in boxes) are the words in cartoons
- scenes or pictures are the words the reader doesn't see (set the scene and show the characters' actions)
- most importantly, how to respect, enjoy, and encourage cartooning as an art form in the language arts class

Introducing Students to Drawing Cartoons

Two years later, Dan Pettiglio, another local cartoonist, spent several hours working with students, teaching us more about basic shapes; about using a single frame or a series of frames for a cartoon; and filling the space with long shots, close-up shots, and reverse shots. We drew nursery rhymes to practice drawing skills.

I use all I learned from Lincoln and Dan to invite students to draw and sketch cartoons in their journals if they choose to. They know I value those doodles as much as I do their writing. Sometimes the sketches remain just sketches, and sometimes they lead to more polished products. And at least once during the year I ask them to try creating their own comic strips based on a personal narrative. I use all I've learned as mini-lessons. In language-arts classes, I tell several real-life anecdotes of things that happened to me when I was a teen—incidents that seem funny now, but were not particularly funny then. I tell them the story about my mother showing all my friends my first bra, or the story about my sister hiding under my bed when I thought I was home alone, or the story about plucking my eyebrows.

> When I was in seventh grade I liked a boy who didn't even know I existed, even though we were lab partners in science class. He was in love with an older woman, Patty Durkin, an eighth grader. I spent weeks trying to see what he saw in Patty. I narrowed it down to her eyebrows. Patty plucked her eyebrows. After this major discovery I rushed home from school, tore through the Elizabeth Arden powders and creams in my mother's top bureau drawer until I found the tweezers. I then locked myself in the bathroom. I grasped the tweezers firmly and yanked. Again and again and again, until the skin above my eyes bubbled into little red mounds as each tiny hair popped out. Tears filled my eyes. I stared at my eyebrows in the mirror. Still thick and bushy. No wonder he's never noticed me, I thought. I continued yanking

and plucking until a thin pencil-line of hair curved across each brow. I was sure the puffed mounds of inflamed skin would disappear by morning. They didn't. I wanted him to notice me. He did. He leaned across the lab table. "What in hell happened to your eyebrows? They look awful. Doesn't it hurt?"

He had no idea how much it hurt. But it wasn't my eyebrows. At least he whispered, I thought.

It wasn't until months later I realized what it was that Patty had that I didn't. In seventh grade I was still wearing an undershirt. Patty was not. She most definitely was not!

I write my story out. I ask the kids to write out some of theirs. They choose the one story that is the most descriptive and seems to draw the most positive response from their peers to take to Beth Doran Healey's art class in order to create a comic strip. These stories and comic strips count in the art and language arts classes: They draw and write in both classes.

Comic strips have their roots in caricature and political satire. Asking kids to draw their own cartoons, after showing them examples of humorous and political cartoons, helps them pay attention to the message of this art form. My whole-class instructional lessons are drawn from all I learned from Lincoln and Dan, and include showing them examples from Peanuts, Calvin and Hobbes, Big Nate, and numerous political cartoons. We talk about all they notice and what they think the point is: "What do you see? What do you make of this? What does it mean to you? What do you think the author is trying to get across?"

After they write their stories I ask, "Can you draw what you've described?" In order to draw what they write, students have to be clear and concise. The visual format encourages them to show, not tell. Once the cartoon is drawn, they notice that design and color really grab a reader's attention. Students quickly realize also that the best cartoons convey a message—whether it's humorous, serious, or satirical.

I've found, too, that writing these vignettes or humorous stories lets kids laugh at themselves and some of the things we take too seriously in life. Dave Barry's essays provide wonderful vignettes for students to turn into comics, as well as their own life stories. I also read the story "Tomato on the Brain" (*Writers Inc Sourcebook*, 1995, 8) to them, and other humorous personal reminiscences from other students so they "get the picture." (Please see Sara's and Mike's cartoons on the accompanying CD.)

Another possiblity is to ask students to collaborate on a story. One student draws what someone else has written. It is another useful way to get the writer to be descriptive and thorough. Students who have a difficult time drawing appreciate the way someone else brings their stories to life.

Expanded Journal Entry

I encourage students to expand a sketch or cartoon into a polished piece of drawing. I noticed Adam doing more sketching than writing in his journal and pushed him to consider turning some of his distaste for writing and love of drawing into a finished piece. He expanded his one sentence, "I'd rather be doing anything, than writing . . ." to "I hate writing more than, more than, . . . being sat on by a sumo wrestler." At each conference, he told me more about what he'd rather have happen to him than write. He crafted a poem and illustrated each point.

I was amazed at the time he spent redrafting drawings. When I asked him to tell me why the first drawings weren't good enough, he explained they didn't look "mean" or "scary" enough. They were too "cartoony" and he wanted them to be more serious, even if they were meant to be funny. He wanted to show he really did hate writing, so his sketches had to be funny and serious. "They have to show he means he hates it that much."

Comparing Adam's first-draft sketch to the finished product, his collection of drawings and poem made into a poster, clearly illustrates how many changes his drawings went through as he rethought what he wanted to convey.

Adam was right; his sketches did become more serious, yet maintained a sense of humor.

Adam became an expert on drawing and sketching. I wanted him to grow as a writer, but I also wanted him to develop his strengths as an artist by using both forms of communication to show us what he knew and thought.

Adam's first-draft sketch.

Adam's I'd Rather . . .
cartoon poster

I'D RATHER SWIM IN SHARK INFESTED WATERS, THAN WRITE.

I'D RATHER BE SAT ON BY A SUMO WRESTLER, THAN WRITE.

Adam's I'd Rather . . .
cartoon poster
(continued)

Jim's Liver!

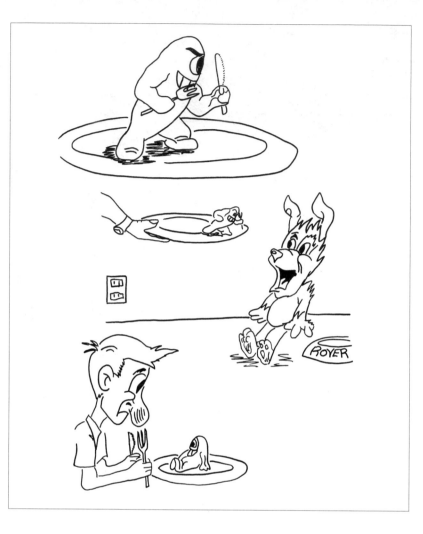

In his journal, Jim mentioned hating liver. He expanded his minimal entry to a fictional story about a little boy being made to sit at the table until he finished his liver. Even the dog wouldn't touch the liver when he tried sneaking it to him. Jim's cartoon characters were so vivid they could almost stand on their own to tell the story. He completed the story by expanding his original entry and using his cartoons to enhance his words.

Cartoons in Social Studies and Science

Students often understand difficult concepts a lot more easily when they can put their understandings into their terms and experiment with a presentation that shows what they have learned. Cartoons let them do that. Sandy did just that when she turned a social-studies assignment into a cartoon.

Dick and Jane visit the Massachusetts Bay Colony.

Dick and Jane (continued)

Corbe presented her understanding of "light," and Emily crafted what she knew about physics concepts when they each created a terminology picture book for their science class with teacher Sue Bissell.

Students complete many lengthy reports, technical write-ups of experiments, and controversial current-events reports in their science and social-studies classes. Encouraging students to find innovative ways—picture books, pamphlets, cartoons, videotaping—of presenting what they know engages them and helps them learn. At the same time, through these varied presentational formats, students are able to share their learning and teach others in ways that more closely resemble real-life projects. Asking them to use information in a unique format also eliminates copying from encyclopedias and the internet because they have to reshape the information they discover to fit their format. And unlike standard school reports, these real-life, authentic presentations are fun to read.

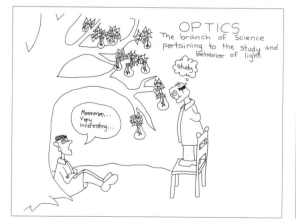

Examples from Corbe's Study of Light

Examples from Emily's Physics Terminology

Illustrating in the School Newspaper

Each of our seventh-grade sections writes an edition of the school newspaper. As part of that process, we teach the students the differences between comics and political cartoons. All students must be reporters and learn to write hard news, op-ed pieces, feature stories, sports articles, and some type of cartoon—either political or comical. Those students on the graphics and layout staff must also design advertisements. Often, we include pictures drawn by students as fillers, to teach them the use of those miscellaneous pieces. I am including a page from one of our newspapers here so readers can see the format and the connection to one of the cartoons. The page of drawings is laid out simply to view all the kinds of cartoons and drawings (comic strip, political cartoon, drawing as filler, and advertisement) that students might do; however, this is not the way they would be arranged in the final layout of the newspaper.

Envisioning a Storytelling

When we are studying myths, folktales, epics, and legends in the seventh grade, we do a lot of storytelling or story theater. We read *The Odyssey*, then choose one of Ulysses's adventures to tell to younger students. (I will say more

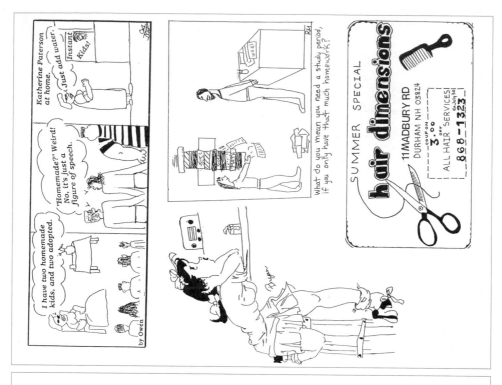

Quotes from Katherine Paterson

Talking about how she gets her ideas for writing: "I don't have a well that I dip from..."

collected by Jon

"The only raw material I have is myself."
collected by Sally and Melanie

"Lyddie is really a part of me."
collected by Janna

"Everything I am is what I like to read.... Who I am is in my writing."
collected by Christina

"Reading a great novel is a conversion experience; we are never quite the same afterwards."

collected by Rachel and Melanie

"At thirteen, when other girls were beginning to experiment with lipstick and making eyes at boys, I was romping in the woods with my mongrel at my heels, feeling that we were Jody and Flag in fact and not just in imagination."
the influence of The Yearling
collected by Melanie

"He tried to figure out later what had made him so angry. Partly, of course, it made him furious that anyone as dumb as Brenda would think she could make fun of Leslie."

from Bridge to Terabithia
collected by Owen

"He reached out, grateful that on that tall stone the name he needed could be reached, and lightly traced the letters of his father's name. The stone felt warm from the winter sun. It wasn't like a gravestone at all. It was like something alive and lovely. He could see his own hand reflected across his father's name. Tears started in his eyes, surprising him, because he felt so happy to be here, so close to actually touching that handsome man in his jaunty cap with the tie of his uniform loose and the neck unbuttoned."

from Park's Quest
collected by Marci

All About Books: Curiosity
by Ben

ORMS. When I first heard that Katherine Paterson was coming to our school, I didn't even know who she was. I went home and told my parents that an author was coming to school. My mom asked, "What did she write?"

"I think she wrote a book called Jacob Have I Loved," I said.

"Oh, I loved that book," my mom cried.

When you think of how authors have an impact on lives with books, you want to read more. I'm going to read Jacob Have I Loved. I'm curious to find out what it's about.

Thank you for coming to our school, Katherine Paterson.

World Famous Writer
by Sarah

Katherine Paterson is one of the best children's writers in the world. Paterson had to make it through a tough journey before she became a successful writer.

She had no desire to write children's books until she was asked to write a story for the fifth and sixth graders who went to her church. She said, "Sure!" she'd do it.

She loved to read books and write to herself but never considered writing books. She wrote the book and realized that writing books was what she wanted to do. So she wrote poems, short stories, and long stories. Finally, seven years later, her first book was published.

Most of her ideas come from problems she had or she knew about. She writes them out and adds a little more.

Paterson now lives in Vermont. She is happily married with four children. She loves writing children's stories.

Newspaper Page and Page of Drawings

about that in "Listening to Language.") We often choose the Cyclops episode as told in the Fitzgerald translation (1961), because there are so many strong emotions—fear, anger, courage, conceit, greed, indifference, tenderness, and more—exhibited by diverse characters. Polyphemus, the Cyclops, is a brute, savage cannibal, an outcast, ostracized by his own father, and yet, in some ways, he exhibits great tenderness that makes us feel sorry for him.

Based on the section a student chooses to tell, he or she must first envision his or her part as a cartoon. In drafting these cartoons I draw on all I learned from Lincoln Peirce and Dan Pettiglio with regard to shapes, sound, frames, and close-ups for teaching the students. We look at Marcia Williams's book *Greek Myths* (1991) for ideas on colors, borders, and characterization. Just drawing their parts out helps the students understand and remember the words. With the cartoon they can envision what they are telling because they have drawn what it means.

Painting Poetry on Walls

Purposely writing on the interior walls of the school: It sends a clear message to students and adults. We value writing. Our students worked with a poet for more than a week as part of a writers-in-residence program that our parent organization sponsored for eighth graders. We decided we wanted to do something permanent with the poetry that students wrote— something that would reach the widest audience.

Derek's part from the Cyclops episode.

Caitlin's part from the Cyclops episode.

Students read all the poems that were written during the residency, picked the strongest poems, and planned where each would look best in the building. We received permission from the principal and went to work. We involved as many students as possible so that many would have a vested interest in the final products. If one student's poem was chosen, another student lettered the poem on the wall in pencil, a third student painted the final draft in calligraphy, and a fourth student illustrated the poem. We painted more than a dozen poems on the school walls, thus involving close to fifty students in the process. I helped students select the poems, while Beth Doran Healey, the art teacher, taught the students calligraphy and helped them design illustrations for each poem.

The poetry on the walls created a stunning entryway into our building.

CONCLUSIONS

Last June, we took a group of eighth graders to Appledore Island, off the coast of New Hampshire, specifically to explore tidal pools and to look at the research laboratory on the island. Celia Thaxter, a writer, poet, and gardener lived on the island a century ago. A replica of her garden still grows on the island, kept alive by volunteers from a Seacoast garden club. We wanted to see it. As we came upon the garden I remember saying, "That's

Karen illustrating Kerry's poem

it! That's all there is?" We walked around, snapped a few pictures, and left. Jessi, one of the eighth graders, asked if she could snap a few pictures with my camera. When the developed pictures came back I was embarrassed. Jessi moved in close for her pictures. Mine were sweeping panoramas in which I tried to capture everything and yet saw nothing. Jessi captured so much more, by looking at just one thing at a time. The flaming red poppies, snow white and purple phlox, rose campion, even posion ivy and sumac thick along the stone foundations. She captured the luminescent blues, and yellows, and reds, even the curves and turns of the petals as they nodded and bobbed in the sea breeze. Celia Thaxter called the garden, "A tiny space of tangled bloom/Wherein so many flowers found room,/A miracle it seemed to be! . . ."

This is how the classroom feels to me sometimes—"a tiny space of tangled bloom"—and it's a miracle to me that so many good things happen. But when I write about all that goes on, I'm afraid I try to capture too much, and then no one can see anything. In selecting examples of students' drawing and sketching to include, I left so many others out: Molly's Moon Quilt, Tidal Pool Quilt, and Anne Frank Quilt; Boris's Web-Site; Rob's and Nick's drawings of fantasy animals for ocean studies. All of them rich and complicated, colorful and elaborate. None of them was easy to reproduce. I worry that I didn't put enough in. I worry that I put too much in.

I use photography a lot to stimulate my writing, to capture a moment I don't want to forget. I'm learning how to move in close. I should know

63

that. It's what I know about a piece of writing. Still, it often takes students to remind me what I know, to teach me to look more closely.

I hope there is enough in here to show that students move in close and pay attention to the smallest details when they sketch and draw. I hope there is not too much, so that readers won't say, "That's it. That's all there is." Impressionist painter Childe Hassam found so much inspiration in Celia Thaxter's small garden. I hope readers can find a bit of inspiration here, if just from one student.

I don't want what happened to Trina Schart Hyman to happen to Kirsten and Adam and Molly. Hyman, one of America's finest picture-book illustrators, was never allowed to draw in school.

> I couldn't ever concentrate on what I was supposed to be learning about, because all I wanted to do was to be left alone, to read books, or listen to music, or to draw pictures of witches and princesses when I should have been learning fractions. After eleven years, I came out of the public school system believing I was a hopelessly stupid little creature who would never be able to learn or to think. (1981)

I want my classroom to be a laboratory for the language arts, not just written words.

REFERENCES

Works Cited

CHANCER, JONI and GINA RESTER-ZODROW. 1997. *Moon Journals: Writing, Art, and Inquiry through Focused Nature Study.* Portsmouth, NH: Heinemann.

CISNEROS, SANDRA. 1991. *Woman Hollering Creek.* New York: Vintage Books.

ERNST, KAREN. 1994. *Picturing Learning: Artists and Writers in the Classroom.* Portsmouth, NH: Heinemann.

EVSLIN, BERNARD. 1969. *The Adventures of Ulysses.* New York: Scholastic.

FITZGERALD, ROBERT (Trans.) 1961. *The Odyssey.* New York: Doubleday.

HYMAN, TRINA SCHART. 1981. *Self-Portrait: Trina Schart Hyman.* Reading, MA: Addison-Wesley.

PEIRCE, LINCOLN. 1992. *Add More Babes.* New York: The Trumpet Club.

SEBRANEK, PATRICK and DAVE KEMPER. 1995. *Writers Inc Sourcebook.* Burlington, WI: Write Source.

STAPLES, SUZANNE FISHER. 1989. *Shabanu: Daughter of the Wind.* New York: Alfred A. Knopf.

WILLIAMS, MARCIA (Retold and Illustrated by). 1991. Homer's *Greek Myths.* Cambridge, MA: Candlewick Press.

Additional Comic Book Formats

AVI AND BRIAN FLOCA. 1993. *City of Light, City of Dark* (A comic-book novel). New York: Scholastic.

PARKER, STEVE and JOHN KELLY. 1996. *Shocking Science: 5,000 years of mishaps and misunderstandings.* Atlanta: Turner Publishing.

SPIEGELMAN, ART. 1986. *Maus I.* New York: Pantheon Books.

SPIEGELMAN, ART. 1992. *Maus II*. New York: Pantheon Books.

SPIEGELMAN, ART. 1994. *The Complete Maus* (CD-ROM). Produced by Elizabeth Scarborough. New York: Voyager.

This CD contains the entire contents of the original two volumes, two hours of audio interviews between Art and Vladek Spiegelman, sketches, photos and artwork, and audio and video commentary on the making of *Maus*.

WATTERSON, BILL. 1987. *Calvin and Hobbes*. New York: The Trumpet Club.

WATTERSON, BILL. 1991. *The Revenge of the Baby-Sat*. Kansas City, MO: Andrews and McMeel.

WILLIAMS, MARCIA (Retold and Illustrated by). 1996. Homer's *The Iliad and the Odyssey*. Cambridge, MA: Candlewick Press.

WILLIAMS, MARCIA (Retold and Illustrated by). 1993. Miguel de Cervantes's *Don Quixote*. Cambridge, MA: Candlewick Press.

Picture Books Combining Art and Writing

There are thousands of picture books that offer extraordinary artwork combined with carefully chosen words, fiction, nonfiction, and poetry. These are only a few of my favorites from the hundreds in my classroom. Sitting in a bookstore or children's room in a library, perusing and listing your favorites, are the best ways I know to begin collecting and inviting adolescents into these books.

ABEEL, SAMANTHA and CHARLES R. MURPHY. 1994. *Reach for the Moon*. Duluth, MN: Pfeifer-Hamilton.

Samantha Abeel, at thirteen years of age, and despite a mathematical learning disability, responds with extraordinary writing to the breathtaking watercolors of artist Charles Murphy.

EVANS, WALKER and CYNTHIA RYLANT. 1994. *Something Permanent*. New York: Harcourt Brace and Company.

The photographs of Walker Evans and the poems of Cynthia Rylant tell the stories of ordinary peoples' lives in the stark circumstances of the Great Depression.

FEELINGS, TOM and MAYA ANGELOU. 1987. *Now Sheba Sings the Song*. New York: E.P. Dutton.

FEELINGS, TOM and ELOISE GREENFIELD. 1981. *Daydreamers*. New York: Dial Books.

FEELINGS, TOM and NIKKI GRIMES. 1978. *Something on my Mind*. New York: Dial Books.

The pencil or pen and ink drawings of Tom Feelings combined with the writing of these extraordinary poets make for superb picture books.

GAIGE, AMITY. 1990. *We Are a Thunderstorm*. Kansas City, MO: Landmark Editions.

At sixteen years of age Amity wrote and photographed this sophisticated collection of poetry.

SPIVAK, DAWNINE and DEMI. 1997. *Grass Sandals*. New York: Atheneum Books.

A simple retelling of the travels of the seventeenth-century Japanese poet, Basho, across his island homeland. The stunning illustrations and spare verses of haiku he composed give shape and form to the small details we often miss in life.

Professional Books Focused on Journal Writing and Sketching

CHANCER, JONI and GINA RESTER-ZODROW. 1997. *Moon Journals: Writing, Art, and Inquiry through Focused Nature Study*. Portsmouth, NH: Heinemann.

ERNST, KAREN. 1977. *A Teacher's Sketch Journal: Observations on Learning and Teaching*. Portsmouth, NH: Heinemann.

FLETCHER, RALPH. 1996. *A Writer's Notebook: Unlocking the Writer Within You*. New York: Avon Books.

FLETCHER, RALPH. 1996. *Breathing In, Breathing Out: Keeping a Writer's Notebook*. Portsmouth, NH: Heinemann.

HARWAYNE, SHELLEY. 1992. *Lasting Impressions: Weaving Literature into the Writing Workshop*. Portsmouth, NH: Heinemann.

HUBBARD, RUTH and KAREN ERNST. 1996. *New Entries: Learning by Writing and Drawing*. Portsmouth, NH: Heinemann.

4 | WEAVING THE THREADS OF RESPONSE
Reading, Writing, and Music

(Students need) opportunity to think creatively and critically about relevant and interesting topics, about things that make a difference, to the individual and to the world.

Smith, 1990, p. 125

It is June—the night before the last day of school. One hundred fifty seventh graders are performing their original musical for more than three hundred parents, teachers, and other students. We are packed elbow to elbow. We have created a make-shift theater-in-the-round in the gymnasium at our middle school. I am behind the audience attempting to keep one hundred forty-nine members of the cast relatively quiet, despite the stifling heat. Sweat runs down my arms, drips off my elbows, my eyebrows, my nose. The lingering odors from years of basketball and volleyball games hang heavy in the air. The audience, fanning the still air with their play programs, watches with rapt attention the conclusion of Scene Two. Dave Ervin, the music teacher, strikes a chord on the piano, as Josh joins in on guitar. Scene Three begins. A dim spotlight finds Matt, a seventh grader who often can't answer his biggest question about school, "What's this for?" Tonight he is playing the role of Rico. It is the 1990s. Rico, a high-school student and the head of a gang known as the Pounders, is alone and hiding in an abandoned textile mill, blamed for a crime he didn't commit. He opens his mouth and sings:

> I sometimes wonder what has happened to me.
> I was left alone, dropped on the street.
> Left to fend for myself.
> Nothing really mattered, not even life itself.
> This is my life. This is how it goes.
> When you live the way that I do
> You get used to the blows.
> When somethin's goin' down
> Some one's gotta fall.
> This is my life, up against the wall . . .

For several seconds after Matt stops singing, I notice that the whole room is holding its breath. Then it exhales into thunderous applause. Matt, too, exhales. It is no easy task, singing a solo in front of one's peers, especially when you have never sung or acted, much less wanted to. And this is no easy song. It is ripe with emotion, laden with high notes. But Matt hits them all. It doesn't matter that it's June, or that it's the night before the last day of school. For the first time in seventh grade, Matt has his answer to, "What's this for?" And not just Matt. As the lights come up, I notice Alyssa and Julie.. They are rows apart but find each other's eyes. They, too, know the answer. They wrote the lyrics to this song.

For years Dave Ervin, the music teacher, and I talked about planning a project together. But we never found the time to design a plan. We missed so many other opportunities believing perhaps that such a collaborative effort required complicated and time-consuming planning. We finally admitted that we would never find the time. "Let's just do it," we said.

For Dave, music is a mode of expression, as writing is for me, that attempts to describe those things that we do not yet understand. In both the music and language-arts classes, we are asking students to raise the questions that a text brings to mind. We ask: "What surprises you? Perplexes you? What do you want to know more about? What does this make you think or feel?" The text may be a novel, a poem, a song, an essay, a picture, students' own work or the work of someone else. In this case, their answers to these questions took the shape of a performance based on narrative scripts, lyrics, and music.

MEANING, PURPOSE, ENRICHMENT

In order for any form of expression to have value, it must be meaningful, purposeful, and enriching. Dave describes what he means by these terms.

- *Meaning* enables learners to make intellectual and emotional connections.
- *Purpose* leads the learner from one meaning to another.
- *Enrichment* provides learners with a deeper understanding of themselves, others, and the world.

Both of us strive to make those experiences we offer our students meaningful, purposeful, and enriching.

I wanted to teach the seventh graders how to conduct research. I wanted the students to learn what they could do as writers working both individually and collaboratively. I also wanted all of us to read a novel together. Dave wanted the students to write and perform an original musical. For both of us, the process of creating any product is as important for the students to understand as the product itself. Both of us wanted as many students as possible to find success in many different ways. Both of us wanted them to have fun. Both of us would guide them through ideas for a story.

In language-arts classes, students concentrated on reading and responding, on drafting and refining a story, on turning a narrative into a script, on the language and actions of the characters, and on drafting poetry for lyrics. In music classes, Dave guided them through the development and refinement of the story, the refinement of the scripts and the lyrics, and setting the lyrics to music.

Could we work collaboratively with little planning, relying on our intuition and trust of each other and our students to guide us? We had six weeks in which to find out.

IN LANGUAGE ARTS

I have two basic purposes for teaching research skills. First, I want the students to learn about something in depth—something that is meaningful, purposeful, and enriching. Second, I want them to leave my classroom knowing *how* to learn.

Choosing Lyddie

For most of the year, seventh-grade students had read books of their own choosing. Although we had read numerous short stories, poetry, essays, and picture books together, we had not read a novel as a whole class. Too often, when we read individually we miss the opportunity to pull apart layers of meaning. We may miss multiple or alternate meanings when we read alone. It takes interaction with other readers to help us make some of those discoveries.

This time, I wanted all of us to read and respond to a novel together. In the past we had read books that featured a male protagonist, so this time I searched for a female protagonist—a girl, one who is feisty despite the odds. I also looked for a book that was new to me, so I would not have preconceived notions of what the book was about or of what I expected the students to "get" from it. I looked for historical fiction because I've noticed that's a genre few students choose for themselves.

We decided that our research would focus on the textile mills during the Industrial Revolution. We would read *Lyddie* by Katherine Paterson, we would take the students to the Boott Mill in Lowell, MA, and we would ask students to conduct research in many different ways. We wanted the students to take apart the layers of *Lyddie* and construct their own meaning through a new medium, one that was unfamiliar to them and me—in this case, a musical.

We had to consider our constraints of time and numbers. We had one hundred fifty students brainstorming ideas for a musical. We had six weeks in which to write the script, compose the songs, practice and perform a musical. All one hundred fifty students would be part of the performance on stage. And we needed to confine the topic for our students' sake as well as our own.

I wanted the students to read *Lyddie* for background information and I wanted them to respond to this reading in more than a personal way. I wanted them to go several steps farther, analyzing and understanding their responses to the story.

Reading Lyddie

Before reading *Lyddie* I asked the students to take a few minutes to jot down in their journals everything they knew about mills in New England or the Industrial Revolution. I often ask students to do this, especially at the beginning of a research project. It helps us frame the questions for those things we don't know and lets us assess growth when we look back at all we've learned about the topic and the process of creating our own product. After just thirty seconds of writing, the students were looking around the room at each other. Their lists were short. My list wasn't much longer. I would be learning right along with them.

After reading the first chapter, I was hooked. I read a few passages to the students. They, too, wanted to hear more. Students bought their own copies at my recommendation. I provided books to those students who couldn't afford their own. I gave the students eight days to read *Lyddie*—about twenty-five pages a night. I asked them to make notations in their books by underlining, starring, or bracketing key phrases or paragraphs or writing on sticky notes, that would be helpful to them in developing characters, writing dialogue and scenes, and understanding relationships or concepts, during this time period. The story for the musical would be theirs; *Lyddie* provided background research. I asked them specifically to note in their books or in their journals:

- personal reaction to each night's reading

    After reading about Lyddie's reaction to Oliver Twist I wrote in my journal: *Heidi took me to Switzerland where I smelled clean air, uncut grass, mountain flowers, snow melting on a cold spring day. It brought me the smell of melted cheese and fresh milk. A grandfather's wrinkled hands. A hug. The good smell of old. Heidi's grandfather was my grandfather. Softspoken. Dunked in the smell of White Owl cigars. Bib overalls. Starched white shirts . . . All this from the cover of the blue book—Heidi—on the bottom shelf of my grandparents' small mahogany book shelf. I liked books but I never wanted to read with a passion the way Lyddie did. If I couldn't read, would I have sought it the way she did?*

- examples of language or expressions that you would most likely not use or hear today

    " 'You want I should go with you as far as the village?' (p. 6)

    ". . . she minded mightily being beholden." (p.7)

- metaphors and similes that described situations, places, or people

    "Envy crept up like a noxious vine. Lyddie snapped it off, but the roots were deep and beyond her reach." (p. 13)

    "Lyddie could feel the rage oozing up like sap on a March morning." (p.20)

    "Fatigue was like a toothache in her bones." (p.138)

- descriptions that stick with you, bring things to mind for you

    "Great catapillar eyebrows crowned his kindly eyes." (p. 13)

"A factory was a hundred stagecoaches all inside one's skull, banging their wheels against the bone." (p.63)

- examples of ways young women were treated, and expected to behave (go to church every Sunday, support brothers at college)
- conditions on the farms, in the mills, in the boardinghouses

In her journal, Amanda drafted a poem about the mills:

> The five story brick building
> is alive
> Hear the groans
> Feel the rumble
> See the building shake
> That's the mills
> Smell the smoke
> Inhale the dust
> all day long
> People screaming
> The heat above steaming
> Despair hanging low in the air
> That's the mills

- things you notice about Lyddie
    - issues, problems, people Lyddie must contend with
    - ways she handles herself
    - characteristics you admire in Lyddie
    - the significant messages you take away from Lyddie's story
- questions that come to mind as you read
    - Why were only boys educated and girls had to work to support them?
    - What did girls like about working in the mills?
    - Why didn't they protest conditions sooner? or more strongly?

I read with the students, often starting each day with a passage I found significant in content or style. We discussed what we had discovered. I gave them time to read, and sometimes I asked them to try a quick-write. Over the course of two weeks I asked the students to write for ten to fifteen minutes in their journals in each of these ways:

- Draft a letter as a mill girl to four different audiences: a family member, a best friend, the overseer, the newspaper, about what it's like in the mills. Jenn wrote a letter:

> Dear Mama,
>
> I ain't written fors a long times. I've ben mity buzy here's in them mills. I likes to tells you about them canals here in Lowell. The canals used to bes clean and sparkly like the creek down by the Stevenes farm. Nows the canal is getting darker and dirtier and it ain't a pretty site. It cause of the dyes and rotton food that people be throwin out. I sees them does

it in the nites. The canal smells liike rotton eggs thats been in the barn to long for abouts a yeah. It was caused by the mills, mama, those devilish mills. They've killed lots women. Someone real close to me. It's so hot asn stuffy in them weaving roms. Thers lint fling al over thee place.

Im comin home soom. I'll bring thee money I made. Then we cud move out west. Papas ben wating for real long times.

Your loving and carin dauter,

Betsy

- Pour out a journal entry as if you are loving or hating your new found "freedom" as a factory worker (conditions, expectations, treatment, hopes, dreams). Ben wrote:

> This plas is trewly teribl. I aint gona stand it no longer. The workin condishuns ar unberibl. Wonse yu wak into them weevin rums the noise ponds threw yur hed. Yu cant even heer nobudy shotin at yu to feet away. The dust an cotin in the air maks it a awfil strugl to breeth. Id giv a week saliry for a breth of fresh air. The weevin mashins ar horibl. Thay ar very danjeris. Just the other day a shutl flew of its trak an hit a girl smak in the hed. Por sol almost died. The wurst part is ther aint hardly no free tim an the job is sow dul. Yu just sit an wach them mashins. Id much rathir be bak workin on the farm tendin them crops. Another problim in the dam heet. I somdays feel lik a chiken on the roast.

- Draft a petition to the overseer about the conditions you can no longer tolerate (make suggestions about how he might improve conditions).
- Read pages 74 through 80 again. What does reading mean to you?

All of this reading and writing was meant to connect students with the time period—immerse them in the language, sensitize them to the issues, feel the emotions of real people. They were sketching out ideas every time they read and wrote, not knowing where or when those ideas would find their way into song lyrics, a setting, a script.

Krista drafted a diary entry for one quick-write. Part of it said: "I shar a room with six other girls. We are so cramped its like putting all six of us into one set of clothing. Wone girl has a cof and won't see a docter. I heer her nite after nite hacking like a sik cow. . . ."

After finishing the book, she wrote in her journal:

> "*Lyddie* was one of the best books I've ever read. . . . I'm not sure if you noticed, but I wrote all of my favorite quotes in my log instead of the book because I treasure the book and I would like to pass it on to my children. . . . This book really gave me a 'flavor' of the 1800s and helped a lot in writing the play. I felt like I really learned something. History is not one of my favorite things to study, but I'm really into what we are doing in L.A. and

music. . . . My absolute favorite quote in the whole book was (after Lyddie crammed the fire bucket over Mr. Marsden's head for what he was doing to Brigid), 'Behind in the darkness, she thought she heard the noise of an angry bear crashing an oatmeal pot against the furniture.' (p.161) It seems that that was what the whole book *Lyddie* was about."

Visiting the Mill

Once students finished reading *Lyddie* as a whole class, I expected them to continue reading and responding in their journals to additional recommended titles (See "Recommended Reading" at end of chapter). This worked especially well for those students who read *Lyddie* in a day or two and wanted more to read. I also read several books aloud: *The Lorax* by Dr. Seuss, *Mill* by David Macauley, and *A River Ran Wild* by Lynne Cherry. As they read, the students wanted to know more:

"How come the girls left their farms to work in such awful places?"
"Were the mills really that bad?"
"How come they worked under such horrible conditions?"
"Why were they treated so terribly? How could the overseers get away with that?"
"Why did only girls work in the mills?"

To help students in their search for answers, Dave and I took them to the reconstructed textile mills in Lowell, MA. After working on hand looms, listening first hand to the deafening clatter of actual machines, and learning about the working conditions, we returned to school. In language-arts classes I asked the students, "What surprised you? What do you want to know more about?" Their answers, in the form of questions, surprised me.

"Do you think the ghost of Lizzie Ryan still haunts the mill?"
"How did they stand the noise of those machines?"
"How did they breathe with all that dust around?"
"Why didn't they protest?"
"How come they didn't just go back to the farm?"

The park ranger who had acted as our guide at the mill had told the story of a girl named Lizzie Ryan. The students remembered every detail. "Lizzie was a real mill girl in the 1800s. She died when she fell five stories while trying to slide down the bannister at the mill for a quick retreat to supper. Supposedly, her ghost still haunts the Boott Mill."

During their tour through Lowell on an old trolley car, students noticed groups of students hanging out behind the present-day high school near the mill. High schoolers seemed to congregate in definite ethnic groups. These groups of older students were intimidating to our seventh graders. For days, their talk always circled back to Lizzie's ghost and the gangs of high schoolers. As we formulated questions for our research, ideas seemed to head in those two distinct directions: Lizzie's ghost and gangs of high schoolers: What if Lizzie really did haunt the mills? What if she could come back to life? What would she be like? Would she fit in? Why would she haunt the mills? How could she come back to life? What would she be like if she did? What would she find today? Were those real gangs hanging out behind the high school? How were they divided up? What are their lives like? Is each gang different? How come the kids seem to be hanging out in ethnic groups? How come they don't mix themselves up more? Are these the great-grandchildren of the men and women who were immigrants in the 1800's? Are these the descendents of the boys and girls who came off the farms to work in the mills? Were these kids new immigrants?

In their research, reading, and writing, the students continued to return again and again to their own questions about Lizzie Ryan and about gangs. The students' questions about conditions in the mills, their sustained interest as we read *Lyddie,* and their curiosity about gangs indicated there was enough interest to sustain their research. In both language arts and music classes, we asked the students to focus their ideas on a story centered on the Industrial Revolution, concentrating particularly on its effect on women in the mill towns. We had no idea how students' interest in gangs might connect, or even if it would connect at all.

IN MUSIC

The drafting of story ideas began in Dave's music class with the question, "What if?" The students' "What if" questions ran the gamut from aliens having root canals in a dentist's outer space office to a former mill worker being born again as a cowboy. Although no "What if" was wrong, only the ones that students could build upon for this project survived the process as the suggestions moved from student to student. The students kept returning to the ghost of Lizzie Ryan and today's gangs in cities. The focus became clearer as discussion progressed.

> "What if an Hispanic gang in 1993 is accused of killing another gang's leader? What if they run to the abandoned mill and hide? What if they hear police sirens and quickly get into an old elevator? What if the elevator suddenly jerks to a start and they're carried into the past when the mills were working? What if a member of the gang doesn't want to leave the past? What if the gang members are expected to work? What if they form a strike? What if one of them is killed by a machine? What if they try to take the mill workers with them back to the present? What if one of the mill workers looks, talks, and acts like one of the gang members?"

The questions continued in music classes for several days until the students created the beginning of a story that featured the ghost of Lizzie Ryan from the mills and connected to . . . the gangs of today. Those ideas came back to the language-arts classes, where I had students break into two groups, those who wanted to brainstorm ideas that had to do with Lizzie Ryan, and those who wanted to discuss possibilities that focused on the gangs. We then brainstormed ways of connecting the two. Once we had the connection, students broke into groups of three to five to compose an idea outline for a whole story. Each group shared their ideas with the whole class; the most popular ideas were sent to music classes where they were further refined.

Once we had an outline (see Appendix P, "Thread of Life" Outline), we broke it into six scenes, giving the responsibility for developing each scene to an entire class of seventh graders.

PRODUCING THE MUSICAL

Refining the Script—Language Arts

Once we had a scene for each class, I broke my students into groups of three to five, gave them a brief summary of the scene, and asked them to write a one-to-three page narration that they then turned into a three-to-five–page script. Each group read their parts as they acted out their scenes. We voted on the most effective ones, attempting to combine the best from each. Minilessons included:

> setting the scene
> turning narration into dialogue
> refining dialogue based on language of the time, character, and need
> writing narration
> writing description
> finding appropriate places for songs
> writing poetry/lyrics
> rhyming
> writing effective titles
> using literary devices, such as metaphor, simile, and personification

Of the six seventh-grade language-arts classes, I had only two of them. The four I did not have worked on this musical with Dave in his class. My entire fifty-minute period with my two classes each day was devoted to researching and writing their scripts and songs. At night, I often took the rough-draft scripts from the other four classes home to give them my written comments, questions, and suggestions. I listened to their songs after school, and offered my response in a similar fashion.

One of my classes was responsible for the opening mill scene; the other was responsible for a contemporary classroom scene (see Appendix Q, Sample Script: Scene 1, and Appendix R, Sample Script: Scene 2). Unfortunately, we had little time to conduct any interviews or read about big-city gangs. In the class responsible for the scene that introduced the two gangs, I did read several passages from *The Outsiders* by S.E. Hinton, and asked the students to listen to the news and clip articles from newspapers for any information about gang-related incidents. I asked them to pay specific attention to the attitudes of the gang members if they could glean that kind of information from what they heard, saw, or read. I also had these students do several quick-writes in their journals, using the following prompt: "As a gang member, draft a letter to your best friend, your worst enemy, a teacher, a family member, and a potential employer about what life is like for you in the inner city."

I cut out every article I could find and posted significant stories. I related a story to the students about why this research (collecting) was so important to understanding a character, especially one that might be difficult to relate to. Victoria Clark, who played Madame Thenardier, the tavern owner's wife in the original production of *Les Miserables*, kept an artistic journal in which she collected every article or passage she could find, from life and literature, related to abusive treatment of children, so she could portray more realistically the emotional, psychological, and physical aspects of such a character. If there had been more time, we would have spent it on reading more about modern gangs—who the kids are, what their lives are like, why they need the gangs, how they talk, what they do and do not value, how violence is a part of their lives. But we had less than a week to finish the scripts. We worked with what little the students knew about gangs.

I believe improvisation would have helped these students even more significantly in their development of characters—their actions and language. Next time, I will ask students to act out a problem they might be experiencing in their writing. We could have set up a classroom scene, or a street corner scene, and asked kids to imagine how kids might walk, stand, talk, and react to each other. I think this technique is also helpful with any piece of writing that runs into a character-development snag.

In writing the scripts, I learned that the language of the characters is tighter and more succinct than in a narrative. Because so much is communicated through body language, facial expressions, and reactions of other characters—those things *seen* on the stage—the dialogue is shorter, crisper, and must move the action forward. Similarly, as I watched the song lyrics move from the page to the stage, I realized that one to two pages of lyrics were more poignant when just a few of the strongest lines were excerpted and used for the actual song. By comparing the song "I'd Give My Soul for Silence" as seen in Appendix P, with the final version of the song "Mill Girls" in Appendix R, it is easy to see how little of all that was written was actually sung. I also learned that the best songs could be moved from one situation to another because they were specific to feelings rather than content. For instance, Matt's song, "Up Against the Wall," could apply to anyone feeling overwhelmed with things going wrong in his or her life, regardless of time or place. The most effective songs allowed anyone in any context to make meaning for themselves.

As we worked on the scripts, I found the most difficult part was keeping all twenty-five students in each class completely occupied with the scripts or song writing. It did not always work. Some students were completely committed to the tasks. Others lost interest. Because there were no props or sets for the production, there was little else for these latter students to do. I asked these students to design and write programs; write invitations to staff, other classes, school board members, and parents; write announcements for the daily notices; and design posters for advertising around the school. In addition I had some students set up a 4-x-8–foot display showing how the musical originated, including drafts of quick-writes, journal entries, mini-lessons, songs, and scripts, so the audience could see the complex processes students went through as they developed ideas. I also asked students to write book reviews of the various novels or picture books we read as we researched. I wanted the students to write in ways that were connected to the musical. I hoped they would write in ways that would teach both students and teachers. (See Appendix Q, Book Reviews.)

Casting the Parts—Music

Once we had the six scenes, we figured out who the main characters were. In music classes, Dave used two rough-draft songs written by the students (one about the mills, the other about gangs), for auditions. Anyone could audition for any part. Every student in the class then voted on which two to three students should get a call-back. At call-backs, the three students from every class who received the most votes tried out using the same two rough-draft songs. Two students from each section, who didn't want to try out, ranked the students. After the session, Dave and I held a closed-door discussion with the selection committee (two students from each of the six classes). We went around the room. We each voted on one person whom we thought should have a major role. Then we listed the best student from each section, based on strength and quality of voice, ability to portray a particular character, and his or her ability to connect with the audience. We followed two requirements: There must be one major role in each seventh grade section, and there must be a balance of girls and boys in major roles. Being fair is more important in seventh grade than always giving the lead to the very best because the best is often the same person year after year. We have to trust that kids will rise to the occasion when given an opportunity that really challenges them. They do.

Scripts and songs were refined and polished like any piece of writing: Readers (students and teachers) identified what worked or resonated with them; asked questions to refine the pace, the accuracy of the language, or the story; and offered suggestions.

Setting Text to Music

Dave Ervin is what he teaches: a musician, a composer, and a singer. He holds high standards for kids, and they know it. He trusts them implicitly, but he also teaches them. He believes that singing is natural in all of us;

that we start life singing, before we even begin to talk. We have to learn to talk, to speak without pitch. Therefore, his job is to encourage students not to fear uttering pitched sounds again. He also believes that music is a language of emotion; the music behind words is there to make the emotion of those words more understandable. Setting words to music means convincing kids of those two premises.

Dave has created a process that helps kids take their words, find the emotion in them, and discover the music that is present.

- He asks students to break the text into word groups, phrases, or sentences.
- He invites students to explore the meaning and emotion of the phrase or word group through speech, saying it over and over dozens of times until they feel ready to perform the line in a play.
- He suggests students add more pitch to their speech, as if they were giving an impassioned soap box sermon. He continually reminds them, however, not to change the meaning. They must only add pitch to their speech.
- He helps students discover the notes and rhythms of the line.
- He demonstrates how to set an accompaniment to their melody.

Once the students can speak their lines in an emotionally clear way, the music is lying there. The trick is to get kids to say the words until they get the exact emotion, which requires a safe and trusting environment. Dave creates this environment by accepting all that kids say and do. Then he helps them see how they could be better. Once the kids' words connect with their emotions, they can begin to hear the notes. As Dave explains, "If students see the text without finding the emotion, it impairs the meaning and emotion of the words. At best they create beautiful words attached to beautiful but unrelated music. At worst, it is beautiful words that are caged within a nursery-school melody, canceling out all real emotion."

In music classes and after school, Dave worked with the students who had major roles. He also helped the students who wrote the songs orchestrate and arrange the music so that it fit the mood, the character, the story, and the lyrics. All of the lyrics, musical scores, and scripts were written by students with our suggestions and guidance. (See Appendix R, *Thread of Life* Song Lyrics; Appendix S, Score for "Mill Girls;" and Appendix S, Score for "Up Against the Wall")

Because every seventh grader was in the production, older students accompanied on piano, guitar, and other musical instruments. There were no props. With twenty-five students frequently on stage, props just got in the way. Students used hand motions, facial expressions, and body language to indicate various props. Costumes were simplified also: homespun for the mill girls, red-and-black T-shirts to indicate the members of each of the two gangs. At various points during the production, slides of the mills were flashed on all four walls of the gymnasium, to simulate a more realistic setting. On our visit to the Boott Mill, earlier we taped the deafening sound of the looms as they were operated. We used the recording to reinforce the mill setting in our gymnasium.

REFLECTIONS ON THE PRODUCTION

The production was not easy. There were many times during the six weeks that I asked myself, "Why am I doing this?" But the production itself, still a rough draft, was testament to the entire process. When that whole room exhaled into thunderous applause for Matt, I knew exactly why Dave and I had committed ourselves to the project. It was for each student—Matt, Rachel, Casey, Jeanne, Jeremy, Alyssa, and all the others who participated.

In *Lyddie*, Katherine Paterson writes:

> "The next day in the mill, the noise was just as jarring and her feet in Triphena's old boots swelled just as large, but now and again she caught herself humming . . . Tonight after supper, Betsy would read to her again . . . there was a delicious anticipation, like molded sugar on her tongue . . . it wasn't so much that she had gotten used to the mill, but she had found a way to escape its grasp. The pasted sheets of poetry or Scripture in the window frames, the geraniums on the sill, those must be some other girl's way, she decided. But hers was a story." (p.79)

For many students, school is as jarring as those mills. Our job is to help them put "geraniums on the sills," to help kids find meaningful, purposeful, enriching ways of learning. We have to offer students all of these same opportunities for responding to "story." Some write, some sing, some listen; they all read. And pushing their thinking beyond personal, immediate responses, helps them understand not only themselves, but others.

What did the students find most memorable about *Thread of Life*?

Jeanne: I remember the deafening sound of hundreds of looms. The sharp metallic pieces moving faster than the eye could follow. The frustration of learning different weaving patterns. I remember the pictures of faces that couldn't smile. Children, girls hardly older than me, risking their lives every day to earn a few meager dollars a month.

I love acting and singing so every play I've ever done is special to me. But this play was different. We created every single detail, every character, every song.

Caroline: I was amazed at how much we accomplished in the six weeks. We wrote good songs and unlike the seventh graders the year before us, we had a plot that came close to making sense.

Richard: The machines were very loud. There were lots of dust bunnies all over the floor. It was also very hot and they wouldn't open the windows because the cloth is better in that hot and humid condition. Isn't that ironic that cloth mattered more than people?

Alyssa: I learned a lot about my classmates. We all became a lot closer. We learned a lot about the two teachers we worked with. I never really knew much about the mills, now I do. Singing made me feel for the mill girls and understand how they felt.

Brian: I learned how to write music with meaning. When you write a bunch of nothings, you get nothing. But when writing something special, and hearing someone sing it, it's one of the most special feelings in the world.

Through reading, writing, and music, students reflected on, and wove together, their responses to literature and all that it encompasses. Like Matt, they found themselves humming. What better response can we get from readers?

REFERENCES

Works Cited

CHERRY, LYNNE. 1992. *A River Ran Wild*. Orlando, FL: HBJ.
HINTON, S. E. 1967. *The Outsiders*. New York: Dell.
HUGO, VICTOR. 1961. *Les Miserables*. New York: Fawcett.
MACAULAY, DAVID. 1983. *Mill*. Boston: Houghton Mifflin.
PATERSON, KATHERINE. 1991. *Lyddie*. New York: Penguin.
ROSENBLATT, LOUISE M. 1983. *Literature as Exploration*. New York: MLA.
SEUSS, DR. 1971. *The Lorax*. New York: Random House.
SMITH, FRANK, 1990. *to think*. New York: Teachers College Press.

Site Visits

Lowell National Historical Park, 246 Market St., Lowell, MA 01852 (Tsongas Industrial History Center)
The Shelburne Museum, Shelburne, VT

Recommended Reading

BEATTY, PATRICIA. 1984. *Turn Homeward, Hannalee*. New York: William Morrow.
    A work of fiction that tells the story of one young woman who was one of over two thousand textile workers shipped north against their will to work in factories during the Civil War.
BLOS, JOAN. 1979. *A Gathering of Days*. New York: Aladdin.
    This is the fictional journal of a fourteen-year-old girl, kept the last two years (1830–1832) she lived on the family farm, recording daily events in her small New Hampshire town, her father's remarriage, and the death of her best friend.
COLLIER, JAMES LINCOLN and CHRISTOPHER COLLIER. 1992. *The Clock*. New York: Delacorte.

The story of a young girl who must go to work in a mill to help pay her father's debts. It describes her life as well as the lives of young boys who worked in the mills. The authors say that they wrote this book so that the reader would think about the changes and problems that progress brings.

DENENBERG, BARRY. 1997. *So Far from Home: The Diary of Mary Driscoll, an Irish Mill Girl*. New York: Scholastic.

In the diary account of her journey from Ireland in 1847 and of her work in a mill in Lowell, Massachusetts, fourteen-year-old Mary reveals a great longing for her family.

DUBLIN, THOMAS. 1981. *Farm to Factory: Women's Letters, 1830–1860*. New York: Columbia University Press.

Nonfiction. A good primary source of information with good photographs of mill workers.

DUBLIN, THOMAS. 1979. *Women at Work*. New York: Columbia University Press.

Cited as "a model of social history" by the *Yale Review*, Dublin describes and traces the lives and experiences of the first women to face the demands of industrial capitalism, particularly with their awareness of community as it related to the labor protest movement.

EISLER, BENITA, Ed. 1977. *The Lowell Offering—Writings by New England Mill Women, 1840–1845*. New York: Lippincott.

A primary source of letters and commentary on mill life written by the mill girls themselves—their first impressions of Lowell, their hopes and dreams for a better future, and finally their later frustrations over working conditions and the need for change.

FONER, PHILIP S. 1977. *The Factory Girls*. Urbana, IL: University of Illinois Press.

A collection of writings by the mill girls on life and the struggle to survive in the New England factories of the 1840's. The book also tells about the formation of the first trade unions for women workers in the U.S.

FREEDMAN, RUSSELL. 1995. *Immigrant Kids*. New York: Puffin Books.

Excellent text and period photographs chronicle the life of immigrant children at home, school, work, and play during the late 1800s and early 1900s.

FREEDMAN, RUSSELL. 1994. *Kids at Work*. New York: Clarion Books.

Documents in fine text and period photographs Lewis Hine's crusade against child labor.

HOLLAND, RUTH. 1970. *Mill Child*. London: Crowell Collier.

An easy-to-read, highly recommended book that tells the story of child labor in the US. It helps the reader understand why mill owners hired children and what it was like for the children to work in the mills. It also tells how child labor was eventually abolished. Good pictures of children working in the mills.

KULEK, GARY, ROGER PARKS and THEODORE A. PENN (Eds.). 1982. *The New England Mill Village, 1790–1860*. Cambridge, MA: MIT Press.

This book is a good record of the daily life of the mill worker, and includes letters from mill workers, help wanted ads, records of expenses, work contracts, and regulations set down by the companies.

LARCOM, LUCY. 1961. *A New England Girlhood*. Gloucester, MA: Peter Smith.

A good description of Larcom's everyday life in New England before she worked in the mills and after the family's move to Lowell, where her mother ran a boardinghouse and she went to work as a mill operative.

LORD, ATHENA. 1981. *A Spirit to Ride the Whirlwind*. New York: Macmillan.

The fictional story of a twelve-year-old girl who works in the Lowell mill and whose mother runs a boardinghouse. Her experiences help the reader understand the development of the labor movement.

ROBINSON, HARRIET H. 1976. *Loom and Spindle*. Kailua, HI: Press Pacifica.

This is the often-humorous memoir of Harriet Hanson Robinson, who went to work in the cotton mills of Lowell, MA, at the age of ten, in 1835. It is filled with the spirit of accomplishment and freedom that came with cash wages to young women who otherwise might have stagnated on backwoods farms.

SELDEN, BERNICE. 1983. *The Mill Girls*. New York:

The biographies of three women—Lucy Larcom, Harriet Hanson Robinson, and Sarah G. Bagley—who lived and worked in the mills, and later became active in the Ten Hour Movement, as well as the women's suffrage movement.

WEISMAN, JOANNE B. (Ed.). 1991. *The Lowell Mill Girls: Life in the Factories*. Lowell, MA: Discovery Enterprises.

From the Perspectives on History Series this is a collection of essays and historical fiction that presents different perspectives on the history of Lowell's female operatives in the 1840's.

ZAROULIS, NANCY. 1993. *Call the Darkness Light*. New York: Soho Press.

Historical fiction describing one young woman's passionate struggle for independence in nineteenth-century America.

ZIMILES, MARTHA and MURRY. 1973. *Early American Mills*. New York: Clarkson N. Potter.

The authors have included wonderful pictures of mills, some of them still in operation, some abandoned. Some pictures show how the buildings are being used today. There are also help wanted ads for young workers, a map of mill locations in New England, and a glossary of terms.

5 | LISTENING TO LANGUAGE

They live in sound, always in noise. Perhaps because it is so constant, the art of listening to them falls off, and so many things they say are not heard, are swallowed in the overall sound.   (Paulsen, 1996, p.6)

A middle-school hallway? An eighth-grade classroom? Ask any teacher of adolescents and they would swear that the author is describing a middle school setting. But these sounds are from Gary Paulsen's *Puppies, Dogs, and Blue Northers*. Adolescents, too, "live in sound, always in noise." It's exactly why I try to focus this sound, so they can use their voices in constructive ways.

For the same reasons I may not build a rain forest every year, Dave Ervin and I don't guide the students through an original musical every year either. But there are other, less-complicated ways to honor voice in the language-arts class. Here are just a few of the ways.

SONGWRITING

Students are required to produce three to five pages a week of rough-draft writing, taking two pieces to final draft every six weeks. Sometimes there are parameters to the kinds of writing, sometimes there are not. I encourage the students to teach me what they know about song writing, either just for themselves or because they are writing songs in music classes. In either case, I try to help them with the lyrics, in the same way I respond to any piece of writing (pointing out lines that stuck with me, asking questions, giving suggestions).

Amanda turned a poem that she began writing in sixth grade, and finished in eighth grade, into a song when her friends said it sounded like lyrics. She wrote the melody to go with the words. She said, "I remember sitting on my bed crying because Meghan and I were in a fight. She said I was trying too hard to be grown up. That's why I wrote this."

> Have you forgotten the language you knew
> when you were oh, so small,
> the language of the tiny ant and of the tree so tall?
> Have you forgotten what it's like
> to float among the clouds, to ride the wind on silver wings

and to shout so loud that it echoes across the river
which runs to meet the sea and there all that you forgot
is waiting—patiently?
Have you forgotten what your youth was like
and what you did do then, the running and laughing
and playing till dark, with your favorite friend?
                         Chorus
Have you forgotten the feeling you get
when you dine with a fairy friend
when you gaze upon the stars at midnight
and when you play pretend?
                         Chorus
Have you forgotten how it feels
to walk 'cross new-fallen snow
to sip from a birch-bark cup and to see
your first rainbow?
                         Chorus
. . . and there all that you have forgot
still waits . . . patiently.

When Rob needed a song for the musical they were writing in music classes, a play called *Time Flies*, and couldn't make any of his drafts work, I began playing with lines and ideas. His character was a young immigrant who had escaped from Poland during World War II. I had a couple of verses but couldn't get the chorus right. On a camping trip for the eighth graders, Dave Ervin and I sat on the farmhouse porch, brainstormed lines, and finished the song.

First came the pounding at our door—Why do people have so much hate?
Papa dragged across the floor—Who chooses our fate?
Marched like a beggar, a tramp—Will Papa live? Will Papa die?
Behind barbed wire in a ghetto or camp—How can people believe the lies?
                         Chorus
My life was broken, shattered and shocked,
    broken forever on Kristal Nacht.
I try to pick up the pieces. I try to hold on to my life.
The life that was broken, shattered, and shocked.
I'm running now, taunted and mocked,
    broken forever on Kristal Nacht.
Hidden in that wagon, covered in hay—Why couldn't Papa and Mama flee?
An escape from Poland was the only way—Now all alone, how can I be free?
I thought prejudice was only over there—
    Who allows others to act on their hate?
But now I find it's everywhere—I can't look back 'cause it may be too late.
                         Chorus

I was listening to Rob sing the lines I had composed when I realized that insisting on student writers reading their own work in class might not be the most productive way to share. Authors don't accompany their books. Song writers don't necessarily perform their own songs.

As Rob sang my lyrics, he made me believe he *was* a young immigrant, alone, his entire family gone or left behind, and the brunt of extreme cruelty. Lines I had written and heard moved me in an unimagined way. I had to make those same things happen in the classroom.

READING ONE'S OWN OR OTHERS' WRITING

In the process of drafting, I ask writers to read their own writing aloud to themselves, to me, or to their peers. I want them to listen to their words as they draft until they make sense. For the final product, I now let students decide whether they will read their writing out loud or someone else will. Whoever reads a piece of someone else's writing must be familiar enough with it to present it fluently, and in any innovative way he or she chooses. The reader may choose to read a piece of writing alone or bring in other readers if there are several characters. They may present a poem in several voices or with musical accompaniment. Writers need to hear their work interpreted and presented in a variety of ways. It lets them see all the ways readers bring meaning to, and take meaning from, their words. (Please listen to the samples on the accompanying CD.)

TEACHING THE CLASS

As the year progresses, I start turning over some of the whole class teaching to the students. At the beginning of class a student might present a vocabulary word on a projection screen. He or she reads the word in context, defines it, and has students copy down the sentence and meaning. This puts kids in front of the class in a nonthreatening way. They have an overhead from which to speak. They are the experts, pointing out the definition from the context or roots and prefixes. They also recommend books and authors when they cite their sources. They teach mechanics when they mention underlining and capitalizing titles, use of quotation marks, and correct spelling.

I have to be careful how I teach the whole class—kids watch me closely, and often do exactly as I do. Sometimes it's embarrassing.

READING ALOUD

Once a week I ask a few students ahead of time to prepare a passage they want to read out loud in order to give us a taste of their author's writing. Or they may read a poem or a picture book or a short piece they have written.

Hearing the voices of their peers matters. When Savitri, who had not been treated kindly by many of the girls in her class, read a poem written by an Indian poet, her longing for home and all that she was missing became so clear. One of the girls asked sincerely, "Savitri, could you read that again?" They were considerably kinder after hearing the poem than they had been before. They hear themselves and others. They hear interpretations. They learn about language, literature, and themselves.

READING TO OTHER CLASSES

Especially when students write picture books, they like to read them aloud to a younger child or a small group of children. When we read picture books to Barb Rynerson's first-grade class, her first graders wrote notes back to the seventh-grade writers.

John, your PickSures are Awsome
(Dan)

I rilly likedt yor Pikcts thay w'r grit I filt kind Sard wen he floatid away on theice Brg But than I filt Happy wean thay rascowd him
chloe

I Love the illistrashins did a reall ather help you! Liz reat isbook.
like a

Dear Kati,
I re4lly Like your BOOK. I Like the title. I Like This BOOK Becas I Like pandas. I LOVE STOhys That Make Me chy. Did YOU Know That Pandas are NOT Beahs
Best Wishs)
Kelsey

cOdy
I love the illustrashens and i like how you Made the carecters on a stick.
My favret part was wen sammy flow his freinds down
Liz

Dear Katie,
  I loved your book. The illustrations seemed to be inspired by the delicate calligraphy paintings of the Chinese - very appropriate for a book about a panda. Your book has a wonderful but sad message about the dangers of war.
    Thanks for letting me read this.
    Barbara

Notes from first graders.

It's also a great idea to get older students to read to younger students, especially if the older students struggle with difficult texts. Reading to younger kids gives the older students an excuse to read an easier book, one with which they are truly more comfortable, but they might never choose to read for themselves. I always have them practice their read-alouds first.

INTERVIEWING YOUNGER CHILDREN

When we begin our study of myths, we often list those natural phenomena we couldn't explain when we were little. Students choose two or three they're interested in, such as: Where does snow come from? What makes the moon stay up in the sky? Why does the tide go out? Why do leaves change color and fall from the trees? We practice talking to little children three to five years old, and we interview them with paper and pen in hand. Seventh graders then write a story based on the children's answers. If there is a god or goddess in the story, they name the deity after the child. We return with rough drafts of the myths to get the younger children's feedback and to ask them to illustrate the story. Seventh-grade Emily interviewed Chad.

> Emily: Why is it cold in winter?
> Chad: Because the wind rushes around.
> Emily: Why does the wind rush around?
> Chad: Because it lost something.
> Emily: How is snow made?
> Chad: The pieces of cloud break off when the wind rushes around.

Emily wrote the following myth based on Chad's responses in the interview she conducted with him.

> Long ago, when the earth was new, Wind, the sister of the great god, Chad, lived on Mt. Olympus. She had a beautiful, priceless, golden necklace, which she prized above everything else. One day a dryad named Winter saw the necklace and admired it greatly. That night Winter turned herself into a cloud and floated into Wind's palace to steal the necklace. Winter used her magic to turn the necklace into a cloud too, so that it wouldn't be found. But something went wrong, and she couldn't turn herself back into a dryad, or the necklace back into a necklace.
> When Wind found that the necklace was gone, she raced all over the earth to find it, making the earth cold as she rushed. She ran so fast that pieces of clouds fell off, making snow. When Chad saw how much the earth was suffering with the cold, he locked Wind in her palace for six months. On the

sixth month, Wind managed to escape to search once more for her precious necklace.

Chad chased Wind down after a few months and convinced his sister to search only once a year, so that earth wouldn't suffer so much. So the season winter, which is named for the dryad, is cold because Wind rushes around the earth. But when she goes back to her palace, the earth is warm again. But Wind is destined never to find her necklace, for even as she searches for it, she is destroying it. It is falling to earth as bits of clouds.

We make two copies of the anthologies, one for our classroom and one for the kindergarten. The kindergarten teacher tells us the collection is always checked out, with five-year-olds reading, or attempting to read, their stories—the ones that name a god or goddess after them.

STORY THEATER

After reading the simplified, Evslin version of *The Odyssey* as a whole class with the seventh graders, I read aloud, as dramatically as I can, the Fitzgerald version of the Cyclops episode to the seventh graders. I give them all copies of the episode with twenty-five to twenty-seven sections marked off (depending on how many students there are in the class) for parts. They choose three parts they might like to tell, and write a note to me about how they see themselves as "tellers." Their self-perceptions guide me as I give them parts. Ben wrote, "I mumble and I shake like a rattle and I'm not good at remembering things." I made sure he had one of the easier and shorter parts.

Students define words, explain what each section means, learn about line breaks and reasons for punctuation, and begin to learn their parts. They memorize their sections.

One student tells Ulysses's part, and one tells Polyphemus's part throughout. They have large parts—but there are always students who would rather act than write. And they are usually very good at using their voices and facial expressions to tell their parts. Students share all their methods for learning parts. Nick said, "To memorize this part I started by reading it over and over again. It didn't work. I tried writing it; it didn't work. One day I put on a John Coltrane CD and started to play along with it on my saxophone like I do a lot of the time. Then I thought that if I can do it on my saxophone I can do it singing my lines. So I hooked a microphone up to my stereo and sang my lines to Coltrane and taped it. I listened to the tape over and over (it sounded horrible because I can't sing) and eventually I memorized it."

David, who played Polyphemus, said, "I rehearsed my part with my mom and dad about twenty times per night. I looked up words in the dictionary. I worked and tested out different voices, and my mom picked out the one she liked. I agreed with her pick. I worked with my dad on not looking at the ground when I told my part."

Kaitlin reminds us that an audience, especially of ones' peers, matters. "In the beginning I didn't know my part at all! But then we did it in front of our class and I realized that I really, really, really needed to learn my part. So, every night I took my index cards and then tried to memorize it every night. I read it over and over and over . . . until I knew what every word meant."

When we present this episode, or another from the epic story, we have the fifth or fourth graders sit in the middle and we surround them on the outside. As each storyteller rises from chairs circling the audience, to tell his or her part, the audience must turn. Seventh graders practice for weeks using their voices, facial expressions, and simple hand movements to tell the story. They are always amazed at how much they learned, how much they understood, and how well they tell it.

Some years we tell other epic poems, or other adventures of Ulysses, but we always work as a whole class, always connecting our reading and writing studies at the time.

CONTEMPORARY STORYTELLING

Moving from classic stories into contemporary stories, I ask seventh graders to read many classic and contemporary folktales and fairy tales (see "Additional References"). Students choose one story to tell, one that they didn't know before, one with many voices, one that they enjoy hearing again and again, and one that they think younger children might enjoy hearing. They can tell the story alone, using a variety of voices, or with a group of peers, each playing different characters. They go through the same process to learn this story that they did with Ulysses—understand it, know the character and his or her mood and voice, and use voice and facial expressions to tell it, with little movement or acting.

Using a guitar, Kalim told and sang *The Jolly Mon* by Jimmy Buffet. Drew auditioned parts for William Steig's *Shrek* in order to find other students to play the various characters while he narrated. Olivia found three students to tell *The Dancing Skeleton*, complete with Jen on the fiddle. Elementary students love the story telling. The seventh graders learn how to use voice and facial expressions, how to engage an audience, and how to tell a good story.

They learn other things as well. "*Jolly Mon* wasn't really a children's book," said Kalim. "You could read it to a child, but an adult would enjoy it too. The illustrations are very realistic."

"I liked being in front of the class telling the story because it made me nervous, and for me to do it, and do it good, was a nice feeling," said Steve.

"I could create the voices and see the people in my mind," added Kyle. "The pictures were like guidelines. All I had to do was put them in motion."

"I had fun," recalled Drew. "The storytelling was like acting for me. I became Shrek. I was ugly . . . I like to have pictures in my reading or listen to literature. It helps me get an idea . . . It was also nice just to hear the voices [when other students told it] of the stories in my head, like *Knots on a Counting Rope*!"

"Children's picture books aren't as easy as they seem to be. They aren't simple. *Knots on a Counting Rope* doesn't have hard words, but it has a grownup idea to it," noted Tara.

"I liked how everybody really got into the stories," said Steve. "As they told them it was like they were the characters . . . I think things always go better when they're fun. This was fun."

READING A PARTIAL TEXT

I have never asked, and never will ask or require, *all* of my eighth-grade students to read *The Diary of a Young Girl* by Anne Frank as a whole class or completely through. Anne did not write her diary for an audience. Dragging other fourteen-year-olds through it seldom makes them feel empathy for her and her situation. But I want to open the book up to those students who choose to read the entire diary. By reading well-chosen entries that highlight a number of events in Anne's attic hideaway, we capture the interest of many more students.

While we are watching the movie *The Attic*, which is the story of Miep Gies, the woman who hid the Frank family, I stop the movie in several key spots. Several days earlier I ask two or three girls to go through the diary and pick out thirteen to fourteen poignant entries, enough entries for each girl in the class to read one out loud during our viewing of the movie. I stop the movie several times, and each time three to four girls read the passage they have practiced. It is incredibly moving to hear the voices of girls Anne's age reading her thinking. It opens the diary to those who want to read the whole text. It connects the scenes in the movie to the words on the page to the kids in the classroom to Anne herself.

Since I have been reading the diary this way, more students have checked the book out of the library and read it than did when I made them all read the book in its entirety as a class assignment. I can well imagine a similar process with other pieces of literature in other historical settings. It is not complicated and takes little preparation, but gives voice to characters and gives kids practice interpreting and reading in a non-threatening way.

Storytelling evaluation of oral presentation

Speaker: _____ **Evaluator:** _____

Title of Story: _____ **Part:** _____

Give 1 (lowest) to 5 (highest) points for each of the six major categories.

VOICE_____

    consider:
PROJECTION

    FLUENCY

    CLARITY (articulation, diction)

    EXPRESSION of CHARACTER
      (personality through voice, facial expressions, body language)

UNDERSTOOD MEANING OF LINES/PART_____

MEMORIZATION_____

DEGREE OF DIFFICULTY OF PART_____

EYE CONTACT with audience, other speakers_____

POISE & CONFIDENCE_____

Bonus Points (For?)_____

Comments:

                                      Total points:

(These evaluation criteria were compiled as a class when I asked, "What makes a good storytelling?" After presenting the Cyclops episode of *The Odyssey*, we revised the evaluation criteria to include fluency, and poise & confidence. Students take evaluation of their own work seriously when they are given responsibility for devising the criteria on which they are evaluated. When they verbalize what makes something good, they pay more attention to making what they do the best it can be. In order to evaluate themselves and each other, I give four of these sheets to every student before the stories begin. They write their own name, title of story, and part on all four sheets. As they get up to tell their stories they hand me three of the sheets which I hand out to three random classmates for evaluating. Each student evaluates him or herself on the fourth sheet, and answers the questions in this blank section: **How did you go about learning your part? What did you like most about doing this storytelling?** I evaluate the students also and we average all evaluations.)

Evaluation of story telling.

READING A COMPLETE WORK AS A WHOLE CLASS

At least twice during the year, I do read complete novels or plays—and throughout the year, many short stories—with the students as a whole class. We treat these readings like reader's theater, where voices become the characters.

In eighth grade, we drop the writing requirements and read a novel, such as *The Giver*, *Out of the Dust*, *The Outsiders*, or *Freak the Mighty* in preparation for, or in conclusion to, reading and writing about various focused topics. In seventh grade, we might read *Lyddie*, or *California Blue*, or *Julie of the Wolves*. Every student has a copy of whatever writing we choose to read together. No one is required to read aloud, but everyone has to follow along as volunteers read, because hearing and seeing words is the best way to learn how to read faster and better.

This kind of reading works best after modeling a chapter with a few "selected volunteers" first. I then list the chapters we are about to read, the characters we will encounter, and the extent of each reader's part. For example, in chapter nine of *The Giver*, the narrator and Jonas have major speaking roles, mother and father each have a moderate part, and Asher and Lily are minor. I always read a part, and as I take volunteers to read, we talk about the way the character might be feeling and how he or she might sound.

The students love reading this way. I notice that they often use this same approach when they get into small groups to read a common text. They like hearing a variety of voices that carry them into the characters with their tone and pitch. They gain a broader and deeper understanding of characters and themes, and of how reading works when they listen to each other. Discussions become more poignant because readers and listeners seem to get inside the characters as they become their voices. When students feel nonthreatened and have the freedom to volunteer, even the reluctant readers begin practicing parts and asking if they could read as the week progresses.

What we read together matters. I choose writing that is vivid and imaginative as it presents relevant issues or ideas through realistic characters with whom students can feel connections. I choose books to read together that make all of us as readers think and feel, wonder and question, laugh and cry. I choose common readings that give voice to students as readers, writers, speakers, and thinkers. I choose to take the time to read together so students can see that what we are reading and the act of reading itself are so important to me that there is nothing more valuable we could be doing.

". . . as language arts teachers, we are after words, oral and written, but need they be the exclusive avenue by which we arrive at words?" asks Judy Fueyo (1991, p. 13).

In my language arts classroom I am "after words," and it is through vision and voice, both literally and metaphorically, that the students "arrive at words."

REFERENCES

Works Cited

Cabin Fever Entertainment Inc. 1992. *The Attic* (video). RHI Entertainment Inc.

EVSLIN, BERNARD. 1969. *The Adventures of Ulysses*. New York: Scholastic.

FITZGERALD, ROBERT (Trans.). 1961. *The Odyssey*. New York: Doubleday.

FRANK, ANNE. 1991. *The Diary of a Young Girl*. New York: Doubleday.

FUEYO, JUDITH A. 1991. "Language Arts Classrooms: Spaces Where Anything Can Happen." *Writing Teacher*, September.

GEORGE, JEAN CRAIGHEAD. 1972. *Julie of the Wolves*. NY: Harper and Row.

HESSE, KAREN. 1997. *Out of the Dust*. NY: Scholastic.

HINTON, S.E. 1967. *The Outsiders*. NY: Viking Press.

KLASS, DAVID. 1994. *California Blue*. NY: Scholastic.

LOWRY, LOIS. 1993. *The Giver*. Boston: Houghton Mifflin.

PATERSON, KATHERINE. 1991. *Lyddie*. NY: Puffin Books.

PAULSEN, GARY. 1996. *Puppies, Dogs, and Blue Northers*. San Diego: Harcourt Brace & Company

PHILBRICK, RODMAN. 1993. *Freak the Mighty*. NY: Scholastic.

Additional References Focused on Music or Storytelling

BOSMA, BETTE. 1992. *Fairy Tales, Tables, Legends, and Myths*. New York: Teachers College Press.

CLEMENT, CLAUDE. 1990. *Musician from the Darkness*. Boston: Little, Brown.

An evocative story of an outsider in a primitive society who learns about the power of music: its ability to act as an agent of destruction as well as its strength in the face of darkness and despair.

FLEISCHMAN, PAUL. 1988. *Rondo in C*. New York: Harper and Row.

As a young piano student plays Beethoven's Rondo in C at her recital, each member of the audience is stirred by memories.

FRASIER, DEBRA. 1991. *On the Day You Were Born*. San Francisco: Harcourt Brace Jovanovich.

The earth celebrates the birth of a newborn baby in lyrical poetry and beautiful illustrations. Frasier has included facts about the "world around you" and has curriculum materials available in conjunction with the book. She can be reached at 45 Barton Ave. SE, Minneapolis, MN 55414.

GATTI, ANNE. 1997. *The Magic Flute*. San Francisco: Chronicle Books.

Retells the story of the Mozart opera in which the noble Prince Tamino saves the fair Pamina against a backdrop of the battle between darkness and light. Includes a CD with sixteen selections.

GILLARD, MARNI. 1996. *Story Teller Story Teacher*. York, ME: Stenhouse.

JONES, HETTIE. 1995. *Big Star Fallin' Mama*. New York: Penguin.

Portraits of five African American women and the kind of music they sang during a period of social change. Includes Ma Rainey, Bessie Smith, Mahalia Jackson, Billie Holiday, and Aretha Franklin.

KRULL, KATHLEEN. 1993. *Lives of the Musicians*. Orlando, FL: Harcourt Brace and Company.

The lives of twenty composers and musicians, ranging from Vivaldi, Mozart, and Bach to Gershwin, Gilbert and Sullivan, and Woody Guthrie, are profiled in the eclectic, humorous, and informative collection.

LANGSTAFF, JOHN. 1994. *"I Have a Song to Sing, O!"* New York: Margaret K. McElderry.

An introduction to the songs of Gilbert and Sullivan.

MARSALIS, WYNTON. 1995. *Marsalis on Music*. New York: W.W. Norton.

Companion book to the PBS television series. Includes a CD.

MICHENER, JAMES A. 1992. *Retells South Pacific*. Orlando, FL: Harcourt Brace Jovanovich.

A retelling of the story of the musical "South Pacific," concerning the lives of officers, nurses, a French expatriate, and natives on the islands of the South Pacific during World War II. Includes discussion of the original Broadway production and its cast.

MONCEAUX, MORGAN. 1994. *Jazz: My Music, My People*. New York: Random House.

National Association for the Preservation and Perpetuation of Storytelling. 1991. *Best-Loved Stories Told at the National Storytelling Festival*. Jonesborough, TN: National Storytelling Pres.

NICOLE, BARBARA. 1993. *Beethoven Lives Upstairs*. Toronto, Ontario: Lester Publishing Limited.

Through the fictional letters of a 10-year-old boy to his uncle, we learn many true incidences of the "madman" who lives upstairs. Over the course of his letters, Christoph's distress turn to compassion for the man isolated by his deafness and his genius.

Notes Alive! On the Day You Were Born. 1996. Minnesota Orchestral Assoc. Music by Steve Heitzeg.

A story–concert with an original score to complement Debra Frasier's book and showing how the author and composer came to create this work.

PINKNEY, ANDREA DAVIS and BRIAN PINKNEY. 1998. *Duke Ellington*. New York: Hyperion Books.

SHANGE, NTOZAKE. 1994. *I live in music*. New York: Welcome Enterprises.

A poem by Shange combined with the art of Romare Bearden.

SWITZER, ELLEN. 1995. *The Magic of Mozart*. New York: Atheneum Books.

A retelling of Mozart's The Magic Flute, including a biographical section about Mozart and a behind-the-scenes account of a performance of the work by the Salzburger Marionettentheater, illustrated with photographs.

TRELEASE, JIM. 1995. *The Read Aloud Handbook*. New York: Penguin.

WOLF, ALLAN. 1990. *Something is Going to Happen: Poetry Alive!* Asheville, NC: Iambic Publ.

Poetry

MOYERS, BILL. 1995. *The Language of Life: A Festival of Poets*. New York: Bantam Doubleday Dell.

MOYERS, BILL. 1995. *"Welcome to the Mainland." The Language of Life*. Prod. and Dir. by David Grubin.

Video of poets Sekou Sundiata to Naomi Shihab Nye celebrating the cultures of today and the way those cultures have become part of the American mosaic.

MOYERS, BILL. 1995. *"The Heart of the Things." The Language of Life*. Prod. and Dir. by David Grubin.

Three poets who revel in language's ability to reveal culture and history, Adrienne Rich, Victor Hernandez Cruz, and Michael S. Harper are changing the way poetry is heard, read, and absorbed.

Stories for Telling

Over the years, these are the stories seventh graders have chosen the most often to tell. The range of characters allows for diverse voices, a range of moods, and admirable (or not-so-admirable) personalities.

ALEXANDER, LLOYD and TRINA SCHART HYMAN. 1992. *The Fortune Tellers*. New York: Dutton.

BANG, MOLLY GARRETT. 1976. *Wiley and the Hairy Man*. New York: Aladdin Books.

BODKIN, ODDS. 1995. *The Odyssey: An Epic Telling* (Four Audio Cassettes). Bradford, NH: Rivertree Productions.

BUFFETT, JIMMY and SAVANNAH JANE. 1988. *The Jolly Mon*. New York: HBJ.

DEEDY, CARMEN AGRA. 1991. *Agatha's Feather Bed*. Atlanta: Peachtree Publ.

DEFELICE, CYNTHIA C. 1989. *The Dancing Skeleton*. New York: Macmillan.

GREGORY, VALISKA. 1996. *When Stories Fell Like Shooting Stars*. New York: Simon and Schuster.

KEILLOR, GARRISON. 1996. *The Old Man Who Loved Cheese*. Boston: Little, Brown.

KIPLING, RUDYARD. 1986. *The Elephant's Child* (Videotape narrated by Jack Nicholson). Random House: Rabbit Ears Productions.

Showing this video as the students are rehearsing their voices and facial expressions for chosen stories, clearly shows them how to change voices and use eye contact to capture the essence and variabilty of character.

KIPLING, RUDYARD. 1986. *The Elephant's Child*. New York: Alfred A. Knopf.

LUTTRELL, IDA. 1990. *Three Good Blankets*. New York: Atheneum.

MAHY, MARGARET. 1990. *The Seven Chinese Brothers*. New York: Scholastic.

MARTIN, BILL JR. and JOHN ARCHAMBAULT. 1987. *Knots on a Counting Rope*. New York: Henry Holt.

MCKISSACK, PATRICIA C. 1986. *Flossie and the Fox*. New York: Dial.

MUNSCH, ROBERT and MICHAEL KUSUGAK. 1988. *A Promise is a Promise*. Ontario: Annick Press.

MUNSCH, ROBERT. 1980. *The Paper Bag Princess*. Ontario: Annick Press.

PALATINI, MARGIE. 1995. *Piggie Pie*. New York: Clarion Books.

POE, EDGAR ALLAN and GILLES TIBO. 1987. *Annabel Lee*. Montreal: Tundra Books.

SCIESZKA, JON. 1989. *The True Story of the Three Little Pigs*. New York: Viking Kestrel.

SCIESZKA, JON. 1991. *The Frog Prince Continued*. New York: Viking Penguin.

SERVICE, ROBERT W. and TED HARRISON. 1986. *The Cremation of Sam McGee*. Toronto: Kids Can Press Ltd.

SHELDON, DYAN 1990. *The Whale's Song*. New York: Dial Books.

STEIG, WILLIAM. 1990. *Shrek*. New York: Farrar, Straus, Giroux.

VAUGHAN, MARCIA K. 1984. *Wombat Stew*. Morristown, NJ: Silver Burdett.

VAUGHAN, MARCIA and BARRY MOSER. 1995. *Whistling Dixie*. New York: HarperCollins.

YOLEN, JANE. 1981. *Sleeping Ugly*. New York: Coward-McCann, Inc.

Name _____ Sect. _____ Date _____

Rain Forest Research

Animal/Plant/Topic you have chosen to research: _____

Bookmark (May include illustrations and/or facts about your rain forest topic, or an environmental poem, or significant quote on an environmental issue.)
  * purpose: to raise money to purchase the care of acres of rain forest
  * to remind users of the importance of rain forests
  * to use as a placeholder as you read

Due Date: 1st rough draft _____ **final** _____

Research- categorized index cards with collected information
Due Date: _____

Pamphlet
  * purpose: to teach a younger child about the animal/plant
                 to learn about/understand/preserve all species
  * with a minimum of 30 facts (the most unique)
  * includes map where species found
  * sketches, illustrations
  * puzzles, games that answer/inform
  * recommended reading/viewing
  * significant quotes pertaining to preservation of animal or plant
  * references- cite all the resources you used to gather information

Due Date: 1st rough draft _____ **final** _____

Picture Book
  * to inform and entertain in an inviting, easily accessible format
  * fiction or nonfiction (ABC book, poetry, story,...)
  * study all the ways professional authors write about animals/issues
  * study all the ways illustrators enhance and complement
     the written text of a picture book
  * include glossary of words unique to your topic
  * include list of stories, novels, fables relevent to your topic
  * references- cite all the resources you used to gather information
  * use poems connected to your topic as an introduction to your book,
     as an introduction to each chapter, or in any other way that
     enhances what you have to say
  * use quotes that you've found about the earth, animals, plants, issues
     that intrigue you, make you think
  * include an "about the author/illustrator" page

Due Date: 1st rough draft _____ **final** _____

Controversial Issue related to your topic or its environment
* What is the issue? (include the 5 w's)
* What are the pros and cons?
* What is your opinion and why?
* include your page of all references used to research with this paper

Due Date: 1st rough draft   **final**

Group Visual
* purpose: to inform a larger audience of one aspect of research
* in groups of two to three students construct a poster or display that answers one of the following questions:

* Where are many of the major rain forests located (world map) and what are some of the most significant facts about them? (Ex. Did you know...?)

* What is a rain forest? What does it look like? What are the layers called? What plants or animals are most predominant in each layer?

* What unique animals populate the rain forest? How is each important? (Examples: sloth, hairy-eared dwarf lemur, living pine cone, harpy eagle, zombie frogs, etc.)

* What unique plants thrive in the rain forest? How are they important? (Examples: kapok tress, bromeliads, orchids, etc.)

* Who are the indigenous peoples of the rain forest? In what ways is the rain forest important to them, and are they important to the rain forest?

* In what ways are rain forests in danger? Why are they disappearing? Who causes the destruction? Why? (Examples: Deforestation results in... Farmers, ranchers, loggers...)

* What happens locally and around the world when the rain forests disappear? (Foods? Industrial products? Medicines? Air? Soil? Plants? Animals?)

* What is being done/can still be done to preserve the rain forests?

Due Date: 1st rough draft   **final**

What would you like to do for our open house on the rain forest? Write "plaques" on the walls describing various plants and animals? Write and deliver invitations to classrooms and the community? Make "rain forest foods"? Role-play in a skit? Be a tour guide to parents or elementary children? Read a picture books? Face paint? Sell food or bookmarks? List your first three choices and describe why you would be good at that job.

THE MACAW

SAVE THE RAINFOREST!

Do your part for mankind!

If you call 1-800-222-5312, it'll reach the Arbor Day Foundation, and give them $10.00. Your $10.00 will save 2,500 square feet of rainforest.

By Brian

READ: The Rainforest Book by Scott Lewis (Living Planet Press, 1990)

THE RAINFOREST

SOME FACTS:
• Before people, 4% of the rainforest covered the earth
• Now 2% of the rainforest covers the earth
• At this rate we're killing the rainforest it'll be gone in 60 years
• Once the rainforest is gone it'll never grow back, it'll turn into a desert
• 50% of the wildlife on earth lives in the 2% of rainforest
• Even some plants and animals that haven't yet been found live there
• 96,000 square feet of rainforest are burned daily
• In 20 minutes the size of 10 city blocks in the rainforest is burned

RELATIVES:
- Among the largest parrot
- 315 species
- Also a relative to the cockatoo

KILLERS:
- Hunters shoot macaws for their feathers
- People cut down the trees that macaws live in

UNSCRAMBLE THE WORDS

What's relative to the parrot and cockatoo?
AMSWCA = _____
What's a macaw?
DIBR = _____
What's the macaw killed for?
TEAHFRES = _____
What do macaws eat?
SNTU = _____

hooked sharp
strong beak

Long tail

bottom view of foot

- Beautiful red, green, white, yellow and blue colored feathers
- Long tail
- Pointed tongue
- 12"–39" long (with tail)

DIET:
- Wild fruits
- Nuts
- Seed

LIFE:
- Can live up to 110 years

UNIQUE BEHAVIORS
- Eats with feet
- Can be taught to talk
- Climbs with feet and South beak

HABITAT
- Lives in holes in the Kapok tree
- Lives in the Central and South American rainforest
- Lives in the understory

PHYSICAL DESCRIPTION:
- Strong, sharp, hooked beak
- Pointing wing
- Three toes on each foot

jaguar

ENDANGERED SPECIES

Mike

Read the book *Jaguarundi*
by Virginia Hamilton
(1995, The Blue Sky Press)

*Rundi Jaguarundi stalks
in the blue-gray shadow of scrubland
at twilight. His coat is
the blue-gray shadow of scrubland
at twilight. Once, this was the rain
forest wild, but years ago, settlers
began clearing the timber. They
built houses and barns, and fences.
Pineapple ranchers and longhorn
cattle herders came to stay.
Rundi stays out of sight.
Always on the move, he prowls, keeps
watch. He murmurs, "The forest canopy
is going. I'm afraid we wild animals
will go with it."*

MEOW!

JAGUARS

DID YOU KNOW THAT......

* a jaguar can weigh from 80 to 350 pounds?
* there are **eight sub-species** of jaguars?
* a jaguar can **kill** an eight foot crocodile?
* it's the only "big" cat that **doesn't roar?** (This is so because the jaguar doesn't have a ligament connecting its voice box to its skull.)
* that some sub-species are extinct except in zoos?
* jaguars can live up to twenty-two years?
* a jaguar's **tail length** is from 17.7 inches to 30 inches long?

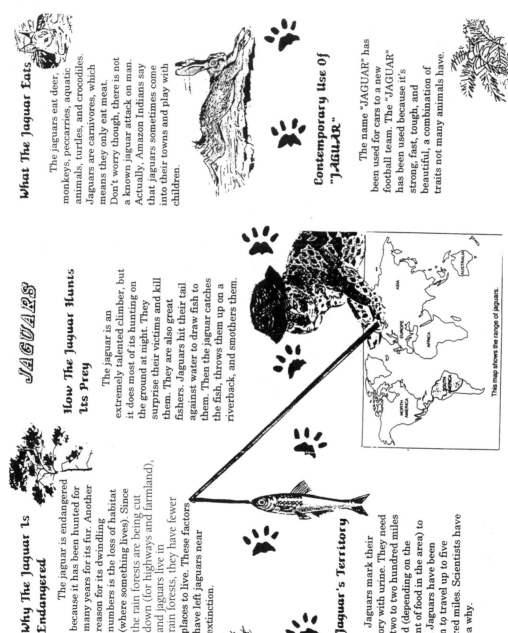

JAGUARS

Why The Jaguar Is Endangered

The jaguar is endangered because it has been hunted for many years for its fur. Another reason for its dwindling numbers is the loss of habitat (where something lives). Since the rain forests are being cut down (for highways and farmland), and jaguars live in rain forests, they have fewer places to live. These factors have left jaguars near extinction.

How The Jaguar Hunts Its Prey

The jaguar is an extremely talented climber, but it does most of its hunting on the ground at night. They surprise their victims and kill them. They are also great fishers. Jaguars hit their tail against water to draw fish to them. Then the jaguar catches the fish, throws them up on a riverbank, and smothers them.

The Jaguar's Territory

Jaguars mark their territory with urine. They need from two to two hundred miles of land (depending on the amount of food in the area) to roam. Jaguars have been known to travel up to five hundred miles. Scientists have no idea why.

What The Jaguar Eats

The jaguars eat deer, monkeys, peccarries, aquatic animals, turtles, and crocodiles. Jaguars are carnivores, which means they only eat meat. Don't worry though, there is not a known jaguar attack on man. Actually, Amazon Indians say that jaguars sometimes come into their towns and play with children.

Contemporary Use Of "JAGUAR"

The name "JAGUAR" has been used for cars to a new football team. The "JAGUAR" has been used because it's strong, fast, tough, and beautiful, a combination of traits not many animals have.

This map shows the range of jaguars.

Evaluation of Research Pamphlet: Writer's Name_____

	(Pamphlet Writer's Own Name)	(Peer)	(Peer)	(Peer)	(Teacher)

Evaluators:

(Pamphlet writer evaluates own pamphlet first)

Evaluate on a scale of 1 – 8 per category.
One is the lowest score, eight is the highest.

Process

	(Pamphlet Writer's Own Name)	(Peer)	(Peer)	(Peer)	(Teacher)
unique presentation of information:					
appealing design:					
carefully organized:					

Content

	(Pamphlet Writer's Own Name)	(Peer)	(Peer)	(Peer)	(Teacher)
unique information:					
factually accurate:					
illustrations unique and informative:					
information diverse and in-depth:					

Consider the following:

facts

literary annotations

suggested references

Mechanics

	(Pamphlet Writer's Own Name)	(Peer)	(Peer)	(Peer)	(Teacher)
sentence variety:					
careful spelling:					
careful punctuation:					
clear, concise captioning:					
legible:					

Bonus (please specify):

Three things learned from this pamphlet:

(Research Questionnaire developed by 7th graders for kindergarten through 3rd grade students.)

What sounds do you hear in the rainforest?

How many different animals do you notice?

What are the names of the animals that you know?

What do the animals that you don't know look like?

What did you learn about the rain forest that you didn't know before your visit?

What is your favorite part of the rain forest?

Why do you think its important to preserve the rain forest?

Please color this rain forest the colors you remember best from our rain forest.

LUKE DuBOIS

Using the pamphlets on the wall, fill in the correct answers.
Rain Forest Facts

Rain forests cover less than ___% of the world's surface, but ___% of the world's plants and animals live there.

In an area the size of a playground, you can find 750 kinds of _____, 1200 kinds of _____. In one single tree in the rain forest, you can find ____ kinds of beetles.

Once they are cut down, rain forests _____ grow back. The land is only good for farming for two to three years. Then it becomes desert.

Each year areas of rain forest twice the size of _____ are destroyed. All the rain forests in the world may be gone in ____ years. _____ acres of rain forest are burned every day!

The rain forests are 140 _____ years old.

Rain forests may hold cures for _____ and _____, two of the world's worst diseases.

When we lose the rain forests we lose much of the _____ we breathe.

Animal Facts
New World Monkeys by Jeanne

Many animals contribute to the noise of the rain forest (not rock and roll) but the _____ is the loudest. They can chatter, squeak, roar, howl, bark and/or whistle for warning or to mark territory.

The_____uses its voice instead of fighting. If two groups of _____meet, they sit and_____at each other. Eventually one of the groups goes away.

Parakeets by Krista

The word parrot means _____. Parakeets are known to repeat things. If a person says a word over and over the bird will usually repeat it. Parakeets are one of the world's_____birds.

The Hippopotamus by Larisa

Hippopotamus is a_____word. Hippo means_____. Potamus means _____.

Did you know that the hippo sweats_____sweat; that some of the hippos' teeth each weigh up to_____; that the hippo can float,sink, swim, dive, and run on the bottom of the water at_____miles per hour?

The Toucan by Amanda

Toucans are one of the world's most _____birds. Its only enemy is the

_____.

Unusual facts:

1._____

2._____

3._____

4._____

5._____

Marmoset by Julie

A marmoset's tail is_____inches long. It eats _____,_____, and

tree _____.

The Okapi by Sarah

The okapi is the only living relative of the_____. Yet, it resembles

a _____.The okapi has a fairly long supple neck and can turn its

head to_____every part of its body.

The Living Pine Cone by Daniela

The long-tailed tree_____lives in the_____of the African and South

Asian_____. Its name means_____because it rolls up into an

armored ball when it is in_____. They feed on_____and_____.

Since the pangolin does not have_____, the ants swallowed are crushed by

small_____the pangolin also swallows.

The Macaw by Brian

The macaw lives in holes in the _____ trees in the rain forest. They could live up

to_____years if they weren't killed for their bright _____. Loggers also

destroy macaws when they cut down the_____they live in.

The Sloth by Tara

The sloth eats, sleeps, and mates_____, hanging from_____.

They have greenish-colored fur because they move so _____that

_____grows all over their coats. Unable to walk, when they do get down to the

ground, they_____themselves on their_____.

They never stop_____ , but they grow so slowly, they never get_____.

   Sloths are so slow, they have been known to stay in one tree for their whole

_____.

Sloths are found in the rain forest _____ (the top layer in the rain forest) of South America.

The Mountain Gorilla by Jamie
Why is this animal endangered?
1._____
2._____

The _____ are the only home for the few hundred mountain gorillas left.

Tree frogs by Valerie
Tree frogs live in an area of the rain forest called the _____. The other three layers of the rain forest are called the _____, the _____, and the _____.

Tree frogs have_____on the bottoms of their feet to help them climb trees.

Poison Arrow Frogs by Mark and Katie
These frogs are only _____long but they are the most dangerous frogs. The
rain forest natives exposed the frogs to _____ and the toxic _____ was used to coat
their _____. They used these poison arrows to kill their prey, thus the name for
the frogs. The mixture of sweat and moisture from the frog's skin is the most
toxin that is naturally possible.

Afterthoughts by Katie
So, what is (or was) the rain forest?
Amazing, huge, vast, thick, moist, high, lush, and ... disappearing.
Sure, you've heard of it, the place where a lot of trees are, the place where a lot
of beautiful animals live, the place that is being destroyed for cattle farming,
housing, timber, and to satisfy the greed of a population bursting at the seams.
Sure, you know that.
But did you know that the rain forests provide 50% of the earth's oxygen? That
they hold 50% of the world's animals and 60% of the world's vegetation? These
forests also hold the key to cures for diseases we haven't even discovered, including
25% of today's medicines. And yet we continue to destroy an area twice the size of
Florida each year. So why not help save the rain forests?

What you can do to save the rain forests of the world:
* Don't buy hamburgers from fast food restaurants that raise their cattle on
rain forest land.
*Ask your parents not to buy rain forest wood products: teak, mahogany, rosewood,
and ebony.

Process Paper (Background History of the Writing) and Evaluation

Name_____Section_____Date_____

Title or Topic:_____

Tell me everything you can about **how this picture book came to be**. (How did you come up with the idea for the piece? What's the process you went through from initial idea to final draft? **What decisions did you make and why?** What kind of problems did you encounter and how did you solve them?) What do you want me to know about the writing of this that I might not know just from reading it?

Please evaluate your process (as described above), the content (What makes this an effective picture book?), and the mechanics (those directions you give a reader on how to read the piece: spelling, punctuation, paragraphing, etc.). You may write on the back of this sheet also.

student grades	teacher grades	comments
process		
content		
mechanics		

Adapted from *Seeking Diversity* © Rief (Heinemann 1992)

Name _____ Sect. _____ Date _____

Endangered Animal/Plant Research

Animal/Plant/Topic you have chosen to research: _____
7 of the most urgent questions you have about this topic/issue:

Aniword or Bookmark
  * cut a piece of oaktag in the shape of your topic
  * on one side letter the name of the plant or animal
  * color the name being consistent with natural colors
  * on the opposite side make a collage using pictures, words,
    maps,... that pertain to your species
  * these are to hang from ceiling to remind us of all species
    being studied so we can share information if we run across it

Due Date: 1st rough draft _____ **final** _____

Research- categorized index cards with collected information
Due Date: _____

Pamphlet
  * purpose: to teach a younger child about the animal/plant
                to understand/preserve all species
  * with a minimum of 30 facts (the most unique)
  * includes map where species found
  * sketches, illustrations
  * puzzles, games that answer/inform
  * recommended reading/viewing
  * significant quotes pertaining to preservation of animal or plant
  * references- cite all the resources you used to gather information

Due Date: 1st rough draft _____ **final** _____

Picture Book
* fiction or nonfiction
* study all the ways professional authors write about animals/issues
* study all the ways illustrators enhance and complement
  the written text of a picture book
* include glossary of words unique to your topic
* include list of stories, novels, fables relevent to your topic
* references- cite all the resources you used to gather information
* use poems connected to your topic as an introduction to your book,
  as an introduction to each chapter, or in any other way that
  enhances what you have to say
* use quotes that you've found about the earth, animals, plants, issues
  that intrigue you, make you think
* include an "about the author/illustrator" page

Due Date: 1st rough draft _____ **final** _____

Controversial Issue related to your animal or its environment
* What is the issue? (include the 5 w's)
* What are the pros and cons?
* What is your opinion and why?
* include your page of all references used to research with this paper

Due Date: 1st rough draft _____ **final** _____

Ecology Anthology
    In groups of two to three students you will construct a "newspaper page" to inform, persuade, and entertain your readers in regard to your topic or issue. We will learn how to write the following: hard news, feature story, op-ed, informational sketches, humorous and politicial cartoons, as you continue researching, reading, and writing about your topic.
    You will rough draft ideas for all of the above. You choose the piece that you believe represents your strongest writing to take to final draft and to take to your group for publication on your group page.

What kinds of writing have you tried?_____

Which piece/s do you want to take to final draft?_____

Due Date: 1st rough draft _____ **final** _____

THE POND IN MY CLASSROOM: ALEXIS' PICTURE BOOK

Alexis introduced her story with a vignette called "The herons" from a fourteen-year-old from Uruguay.

"I remember the day when they came, the white herons and the large pink flamingoes.

"They flocked over our beach house and came to rest on the sea shore. We counted eighty herons. They looked lost and hesitant. Before sunset they took flight again, southwest over the sea towards the big cities. I know they were escaping from the northern lagoons, their home for thousands of years, now transformed into rice-fields. "I often wonder what became of them. I hope that somewhere in the world, a place untouched by man, they may find the peace they lost." Soledad Genta (Exley, 1985)

The Pond in my Classroom
by Alexis

I was sitting at my desk in school, when the teacher opened up a book about birds for reading time. The words didn't interest me. As her voice droned on and on, my mind began to wander. Then something peculiar happened . . .

. . . As she turned the page, water began dripping . . . dripping from the book. Water gushed and flowed onto the floor. I watched with amazement. She turned another page . . . a frog sprang onto my desk. Mosquitoes and dragonflies buzzed about my head. Reeds sprouted and sprawled from the page. Lilly pads and cattails shot up through the floor. Snakes squeezed out through the binding, slithering and sleaking away. Fish flapped about, and birds circled round and round. School chairs blasted up and grew into trees. The chalk board formed into blossoming green bushes.

But I was the only one who seemed to notice. The water rose up to my waist, then swallowed my shoulders and ears. It rose right over my head. I was sitting on the bottom of the sea, blowing bubbles through my nose. A school of bright yellow and orange fish swam over to me, and waved their tails.

I swam to the surface and crawled ashore. A great white bird swooped down to me. He waved with his wing for me to hop on. I climbed on his back and hugged tight round his neck. We sped off like a dynamite dolphin. The great bird, who I knew was a heron, soared and dipped and swung through the sky, with me on his back.

"Faster! Faster!" I cried. My friend beat his wings harder. "Do flips!" I rang out. We twirled through the sky, over tree tops, under clouds, and through bridges. We shot straight down like a speeding rocket. My feet splashed through the waves as he skimmed the water.

The wind blew against my face as we graciously flew along with a flock of Canadian geese. "Well, hello," I yelled out. They honked back in reply.

"Now, heron, fly really high up into the clouds so I can touch . . ."

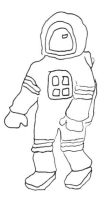

"Oliver! Who were you just talking to? You know you aren't supposed to be talking." I was back in the classroom, back at my desk. "Now go out in the hall and wait till I tell you to come back in.

I got out of my seat and headed for the door. Swish . . . swosh . . . swish . . . swosh. What was that noise? Then my teacher began reading again. "Now, for our second book, we will read about space." Then I heard my teacher call my name. I wasn't quite sure what she was saying. "Oliver, is that. . . is that seaweed wrapped around your legs?! Why are your shoes wet?!" I didn't have an answer because it was happening again. The classroom was gone, and I . . . I . . was walking on the moon.

—Exley, Richard and Helen (Eds.). 1985. *My World Nature*. Lincolnwood, IL: Passport Books.

John writes:

Polar bears are an endangered species because their number ranges from two thousand to three thousand in the Arctic region. Their number has decreased mainly because humans are killing them for different reasons. The main reasons are:

- Eskimos kill them for food in order to survive.
- People in the Arctic villages kill bears on sight when they come too close to the village.
- Hunters kill the bears simply for sport.

I can understand why Eskimos need polar bear meat and hides for their survival in the Arctic wilderness. If this was the only reason polar bears were killed, I do not think they would be on the endangered species list.

The number of bears being killed when they come too close to villages could be lowered. In the book *Kingdom of the Ice Bear*, the number of bears killed for this reason has increased. The book suggests there are ways of teaching the bears to stay away from the villages. One method is to shoot them with a plastic projectile. This will not kill the bear. It will only hurt them, and hopefully this will teach them to stay away.

The third reason polar bears are being killed is by hunters. This is barbaric. To kill these magnificent Kings of the Arctic for no good reason is terribly wrong. Hunters who kill for self-satisfaction should be outlawed from this region. They should be severely punished if they ignore the hunting ban. Hunting bans should be strongly enforced to prevent this type of cruelty. Maybe just by the action of banning hunters polar bears could be then taken off the endangered list and taught to stay away from villages.

REFERENCES

Hinshaw, Dorothy. 1980. *Bears of the World*. USA: Holiday House.
Miles, Hugh and Mike Salisbury. 1985. *Kingdom of the Ice Bear*. Austin, TX: University of Texas Press.
Osteen, Phyllis. 1966. *Bears Around the World*. New York: Howard McCann.
Time Life. 1977. *Bears and Other Carnivores*. New York: Vineyard Books.

Volume 1 June 19,

Cover by Nika, Meghan, and Adam I

Polaris Pages

ORMS Students Visit Bison Farm
by Molly

Durham- "Look at 'em," utters Amanda Michaels, 13, as she and 49 of her peers ride by a herd of bison at the Little Bay Buffalo Farm in Durham.

On the 23rd of May, Judy George and Linda Rief took their seventh grade classes on a visit to David Langley's buffalo farm (actually *bison* as we learned later).

On a mission to seek out the unknown world of endangered animals, these kids have come to learn from Langley, owner and founder of Little Bay Buffalo Farm, and a natural sciences major.

With their new found knowledge and view on life, the world, and non-smelly bison doo-ddo, they hope to use these things to create a series of brochures, children's books, and evantually a whole newspaper about different endangered animals from New England.

Are the Buffalo Extinct?
by Chris

"Where have all the buffalo gone?"

Many hundreds of years ago buffalo were everywhere, from New Mexico to Missouri. The Native Americans hunted only a few buffalo at a time. They used every part of the buffalo: the brain for tanning, the skin for clothing, and the bones for weapons. Then one dark day, the white man came. He killed thousands of buffalo at once for what he called "sport."

But, because of the efforts of David Langley and many others, the buffalo have been saved from extinction. They have saved them by setting up farms like "Little Bay Buffalo Company" here in Durham, NH. And they have passed laws to save this great American icon.

The buffalo have been here longer than we have, so it is only fitting that we allow them to take back their land. But much more must be done before we can truly say that the buffalo are safe.

David Langley: Naturalist
by Patrick

David Langley first became interested in the American bison as a child, when he first decided that he wanted to have one as a pet. At first his mother didn't reply, hoping that her son would forget the idea and become interested in something else.

But Langley kept bothering his mother about his desire to have the odd buffalo, or two, as pets. At this Langley's mother was forced to turn him down, telling him that she didn't want him to have a bison as a pet because she was afraid that she would end up taking care of the bison, which is a huge amount of work. Even so, Langley harbored a secret desire to aid the American bison in its plight and he carried this desire into his adulthood.

It officially began with a phone call. Langley was then 20 years old, calling his parents to tell them that he wanted to convert the family land into a buffalo farm, one that would run as a business. His parents were quiet for awhile, hoping in vain that their son would be distracted for something that would make him forget the idea. But finally, even fearing that they would have all the responsibility of taking care of them, they still gave Langley the permission to turn the family land in Durham into a buffalo farm, so long as "they didn't have to shovel anything."

David Langley is now the owner of "Little Bay Buffalo Company."

He started the farm with five buffalo that were transferred from other buffalo herds. Over the years he has added a few outside buffalo to maintain genetic variation. He now has roughly 34 buffalo on his farm and has a maximum capacity of 52 buffalo.

Langley's farm provides the unusually healthy buffalo meat to buyers in northern New England. To Langley this is more than just a business opportunity waiting to be invested in. Langley knows that the American bison will probably never achieve the formidable 60 million of them that lived before the Europeans came, but he hopes to preserve the legacy of the bison for future generations. He's trying to prevent another unique and invaluable piece of the natural land from slipping into oblivion forever.

Baby at Forty Pounds
by Mike

A russet colored creature rushes through a field past a gate and playfully up to David Langley. No, this is not one of his two dogs, but it is a baby bison, only a few weeks old. The baby is now an orphan because the mother, also an orphan, refused to feed it. "It's a learned thing," Langley said.

As a result of this, Langley had to remove the baby from the rest of the herd and bottle feed it. Now the baby bison thinks that Langley is its mother, and it runs to be petted and fed. Born on the 5th of May she was named Cinco de Maio after the Mexican holiday.

Baby bison are a light brown color when they are born. They have no odor and neither does their manure for the first few months. All these factors help the baby bison stay well camouflaged from predators in the wild. By the time they are six months old, the baby will weigh about 200 pounds. When agitated, the baby bison can, and will, kick with its front and back legs.

It was amazing how puppy-like the baby was, wanting to jump around and play. If Langley keeps acting like the bison's mother, it might even try to follow him inside his house and eat from the dog bowls. The baby has already eaten most of their lilacs.

Bison are nomadic animals and their average lifespan is about 20 years. At full growth females weigh about 750-1000 pounds. Males are six and one half feet tall and 2000 pounds at full growth. Bison can run 35 miles an hour and can jump over six feet in the air. They are endangered. None roam free in the U.S. anymore, except for one baby bison that lives on a buffalo farm in New Hampshire.

Buffalo farewells

Chris Richards

Polaris Pages

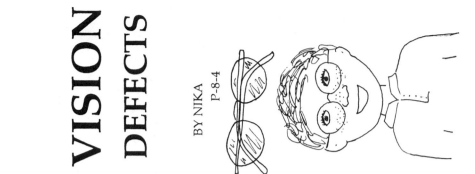

VISION DEFECTS

BY NIKA

P-8-4

Brewer, Sarah. Body Facts. Deloring Kindersley Publishing. New York. 1996.

Crocker, Mark. The Body Atlas. Oxford, NY. 1991.

Parker, Steve. The Body and How it Works. Deloring KinderslEy Publishing. New York. 1992.

Webster's New World Encyclopedia. College Edition. Prentice Hall. New York 1992.

ASTIGMATISM

Astigmatism is an aberration occurring in the lens. It happens when the curvature of the lens is different in two planes, so that rays in one plane may not focus while rays in another plane may. With astigmatism eyesight, vertical and horizontal cannot be in focus at the same time. Astigmatism is corrected by using cylindrical lenses. Astigmatism is often combined with nearsighted-ness.

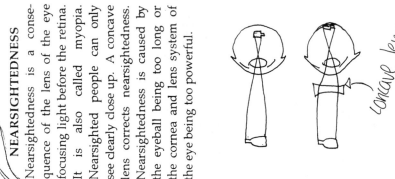

convex lens

FARSIGHTEDNESS

Farsightedness results from the lens focusing light behind the retina. Farsighted people can only clearly see objects that are far away. Farsightedness is also called hypermetropia. Farsightedness is corrected by a convex lens. People grow more farsighted over the course of their lifetime because the muscles that hold the lens weaken, causing the focus point to change. That is why so many people who are about 45-50 years old start wearing reading glasses to help them see close up.

NEARSIGHTEDNESS

Nearsightedness is a consequence of the lens of the eye focusing light before the retina. It is also called myopia. Nearsighted people can only see clearly close up. A concave lens corrects nearsightedness. Nearsightedness is caused by the eyeball being too long or the cornea and lens system of the eye being too powerful.

concave lens

VISION DEFECTS

Farsightedness or nearsightedness occur when the lens can't focus light properly onto the back of the retina, because the eyeball is either too short or too long. The function of the lens in the eye is to form a clear picture on the retina. The lens bends the light from outside the eye so that it comes to a point or focuses exactly on the retina. If the eyeball is elongated in any direction, the lens will focus the picture before or after the retina causing vision to be blurry.

**Orange Is the Starfish
by Kelly**

Orange is the starfish
that sticks to my hand,
sees a crab
in the sand.

Brown is the crab
that likes to hide,
sees a seal
in the tide.

Silver is the seal
shimmering wet,
sees a bird
it hasn't met.

White is the bird
flying low,
sees a jellyfish
down below.

Clear is the jellyfish
that can sting,
sees a child
who can sing.

Happy is the child
who skips along,
puts the starfish back
where it belongs.

Facts about Starfish

- Starfish belong under the classification Echinoderms.
- Most Echinoderms are radially semetric, which means they are the same on both sides.
- Starfish are sometimes called Sea Stars.
- Starfish live on the rocky shores off many coasts. They are largely populated off the coast of New England.
- Starfish have spines on their backs, as protection against predators.
- Starfish can shed limbs, such as a leg, when a leg has been damaged, or as a defensive tactic when something is grabbing at its leg. This process is called autotomy.
- Starfish can move their stomachs outside their mouths to envelope their prey.

Inspiration for this book came after reading White is the Moon *by Valerie Greeley.*

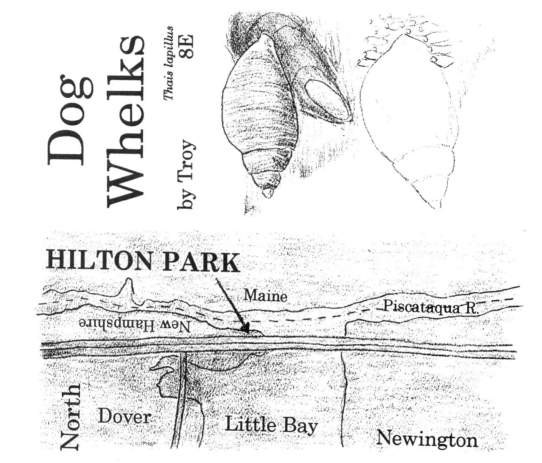

Dog Whelks

Thais lapillus 8E

by Troy

HILTON PARK

Maine

New Hampshire

Piscataqua R.

North

Dover

Little Bay

Newington

The Carnivorous Snail

Two of the dog whelks favorite foods are the barnacle and the blue mussel. To get to the insides of a mussel, the dog whelk must first use its radula or rasp tipped with teeth to slowly drill a hole. It then extends its proboscis, which is like a feeding tube, and rasps out the flesh. To eat a barnacle, drilling isn't necessary. The barnacle's valves are simply forced apart. It is also speculated that the dog whelk uses its purple dye, called purpurin and is highly poisonous, to first kill the barnacle and weaken the mussel holding the valves shut. Dog whelks are also scavengers of the shallow waters.

Reproduction

Dog whelks are single sexed gastropods, either male or female. After mating it attaches leathery, cream colored, rice shaped, egg capsules under rocks and seaweed. There is no larval stage. Each egg hatches about 12 miniature dog whelks. Because the snails are carnivorous, the first hatched snails eat the other eggs.

A Gastropod

The dog whelk is a gastropod. They have a sole-like muscular foot adapted for crawling which moves over a trail of mucus, simple eyes that are able to detect light intensities, tentacles used as feelers, and equilibrium organs to orient the snail to the bottom.

Anatomy

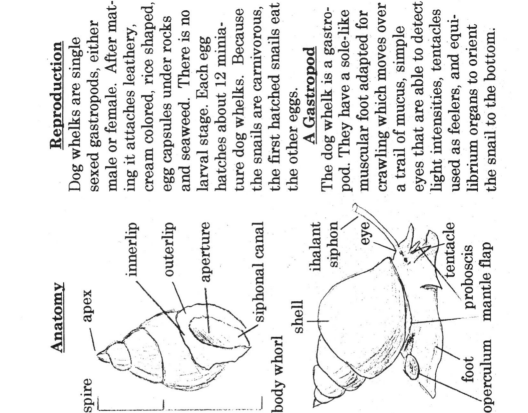

spire — apex
innerlip
outerlip
aperture
siphonal canal
body whorl
shell
ihalant siphon
eye
tentacle
proboscis
mantle flap
foot
operculum

Names

The dog whelk can also be called the dog winkle or rock purple. Winkle is another name for whelk, the prefix "dog" is an old diminutive and rock purple comes from the use of their purple dye by American Indian tribes to produce Tyrian purple for robes.

Habitat and Description

The dog whelk can be found by the thousands on intertidal rocks from Maine to Long Island. The dog whelk's shell is elongated with a point. Its color is varied and usually depends on the snail's diet. Dog whelks that eat barnacles are white; those that prefer mussels have dark shells. Yes, these snails are carnivorous.

Welcome to our rain forest!

You can expect to find a rain forest filled with the sights and sounds and animals of a "real" rain forest. Everything you see has been done by students.

In John MacArthur's room you will find displays of environmental issues facing the U.S., including gigantic paintings of endangered animals on the walls. You will find a display of the process John's 6th grade math and science students went through to create the rain forest and to research other environmental issues.

As you walk through the rain forest notice all the different plants and animals-- their sizes, shapes, and colors. Listen to the sounds. Look up. Look down. Look into and around.

Walking through the rain forest, and on into Mrs. Rief's/Mrs. Moore's room, you will find more displays pertaining directly to the rain forst: pamphlets focusing on animals, picture book readings, "tastes of the rain forest," hand-made rain forest bookmarks (for a small donation to be used to preserve several acres of rainforest), and face-painting opportunities. In addition there is a display of the process 7th grade Language Arts students went through to research and create their particular interests and products.

Beth Doran and Alan Stuart worked tirelessly in their art and shop classes with 6th and 7th graders to create the actual rain forest. Joan Savage and Steve LeClair helped "manufacture" the canopy, the upper layer of the rain forest. It has been a complex, wearing, but incredibly exhilerating experience for all of us. The best part has been watching kids of all levels, varying strengths and talents, work together to solve some very complex problems.

We would appreciate your feedback. What are some things you learned from our displays about the rain forest or about any environmental issues? What did you like best about what the students did?

Thank you for visiting *our* rain forest
Beth Doran, John MacArthur, Maggie Moore, Linda Rief, , Alan Stuart

The Students of 6 OR and 7 JK

Luke DuBois

> *"I discovered . . . that I could so accustom myself to the noise that it became like a silence to me. I defied the machinery to make me its slave. Its incessant discords could not drown the music of my thoughts if I would let them fly high enough."* —Lucy Larcom, 1889

7TH GRADE MUSICAL OUTLINE   THREAD OF LIFE

Scene 1   *In the Weaving Room of the Mills*

The musical starts in a large mill room in the 1840s. The bell rings. It is 5 AM. The girls are beginning to work. Although it's early, the machines begin with a roar.

Song: "Mill Girls"

As the morning wears on, we notice that one of the girls, Ruth, is having a bad day. Her machine keeps breaking, and she knows that this will mean she won't get paid for her work. The other girls want to help, but are afraid to leave their machines. The overseer keeps picking on Ruth, getting more and more condescending as the day progresses. Another girl, Lizzie, becomes increasingly aggravated with the overseer, and finally jumps into the conversation. "Leave her alone. She ain't doin' nothin' wrong. She's doin' the best she can!" He warns, "Hold your tongue, girl!" Lizzie: "It's the lousy machines that keep breakin'." Overseer: "One more word from you, and you'll be dismissed!"

With great difficulty, Lizzie refrains from speaking. On her way back to her machine though, she moves a box (unnoticed by the overseer). When the overseer turns to leave, he trips and falls. The girls laugh. The overseer is unable to blame this on Lizzie, so he leaves angrily. The bell rings to dismiss the girls for breakfast. As the girls in the factory leave, one says, "I can't believe that Lizzie would dare to yell at the overseer!"

"I can't believe that she would dare to trip him!"

"I can't believe that she would dare to climb on the boardinghouse roof!"

Song: That's Lizzie!

All of the girls exit except Ruth and Lizzie. Lizzie offers to help Ruth fix her cloth so that she can still get paid for the day. They begin working, but Ruth is worried that they will be late to breakfast. When the time gets really close, Lizzie tells Ruth to go ahead, she'll catch up with her. "What are ye gonna do . . . slide down the staircase agin?" Ruth asks. "Don't worry, I'll make it on time . . . besides it's only five floors!" Ruth laughs and leaves. Just after Ruth exits, Lizzie's hair gets caught in the loom. As it starts to pick her up in the air, Lizzie pulls the scissors from her apron and cuts off the right half of her hair. When she has cut herself free, she falls backwards and gets red dye all over the other side of her head. She gets up, runs her hand through her hair. At first she thinks she is bleeding, but soon realizes that it is just the dye. When she looks at herself in the window reflection (perhaps window frames hanging in stage front) she laughs. Just then the bell rings again. She tears to the staircase and starts to slide, but slips and begins to fall. (We see the staircase floating up slowly by her, the slides taken on staircases in the mills.) There is a long sound going down. During the fall there is a blackout. (Maybe a chorus in the background could be repeating "Well, That's Lizzie!")

Song: "Weave A Fortune"

Scene 2   *A history classroom in a mill city in New England, 1990's*

This is a frightening and comical place. There is a male teacher (male teacher might not be as interested or passionate about women in the mills) . . . therefore, drones on about the mills. Students are totally uninterested. The teacher lectures about Lizzie who falls 5 stories and how her ghost is rumored to still be in the mill.

Students are preoccupied with something else. (Perhaps freeze frame and no lights on teacher as lights turn on students and all they are doing: polishing nails, pegging spit balls, carving on the desks, unscrewing the chairs, etc.)

Song: "**Reached the Breaking Point**" (Lyrics go back and forth between gangs, trying to outdo each other with how bad their lives are—with a *West Side Story* flavor.)

Classroom students freeze—lights turn to teacher then back to classroom. This time the whispering is more intense. "Is he gonna do it? . . . Don't do it?" The teacher continues about the mills, but the whispering finally leads him to call these two boys out into the hall. When the three are alone, the teacher begins to question them. All of a sudden Rigas pulls out a gun. He points it at the teacher. "Put the gun down!" Rico yells. Rigas points the gun to shoot, and Rico tackles him. As they fight for the gun, it goes off, killing the teacher, who is trying to pull the two of them apart. Rico grabs the gun from Regas and looks in horror. Students from the classrooms and other teachers come running through the doors. They see the fatally wounded teacher and Rico with the gun. Regas and others in Regas' gang accuse Rico, who runs off. Blackout.

Scene 3   *A deserted mill*

The lights come up to show Rico alone in a very dark place. He is at the bottom of the staircase that Lizzie fell down a century and a half before.

Song: "**Up Against the Wall**"

At the end of the song there's a knock on the door. It is some sort of code, so Rico opens the door. Members of his gang come in and tell him that they thought that he might be there. "Things are really bad on the outside. The police are everywhere looking for you. Everybody thinks that you did it. You didn't kill him, did you?" Rico shakes his head. Gang members say they'll find a way out for him. Rico sings refrain from "Up Against the Wall," all the time getting angrier and angrier about his situation (pounding walls, etc.). All of a sudden, Lizzie's body drops down the stairwell. Rico is appropriately startled. Suddenly Lizzie's eyes open, and she stands. Lizzie is a ghost. "Don't worry . . . I kin help ye . . . I overheard ye talkin' with your friends . . . I'd be obliged to prove ye murdered no one." (Injustices of any kind infuriate Lizzie, just as they did in the mills.)

It takes awhile for Rico to calm down enough to listen to her. When he does, she continues. "Will you let me prove that you're not the murderer?" Rico replies, "Of course, why wouldn't I?"

"Well, there be a catch," Lizzie continues. "You see, I'm dead, and well, if you want me to go out and prove your innocence, we'll have to switch places."

"I would have to be dead? . . . thanks but no thanks. That's what I'm tryin' to avoid." Lizzie promises to give him back his life. "I'd be obliged to give it back" as soon as she proves that Rico was not the murderer, but Rico is clearly unconvinced that that is a good idea.

Suddenly a police megaphone is heard. The place is surrounded. "What do I have to do to switch places?" Rico asks.

"Jump from the top of the stairs."

"Isn't there anything else?"

"Well, you could kiss me." Rico and Lizzie begin a romantic bantering and flirting that will continue throughout the play. "Looks like I'll take the stairs."

"So be it."

"I mean, it's not that I haven't kissed a girl before."

"It's just five floors . . . have a nice fall."

"I just have never kissed a dead girl before."

"Perfectly understandable."

Song: "Switch"

The police begin to break through the door. "Don't get the wrong idea." "Don't worry. We'll never be alive at the same time." They kiss and he disappears. The police break in and find only Lizzie (they think she's just trespassing, she looks like a 90's kind of teenager, half her head shaved, the other half red, heavy boots, etc.), and tell her to get out. Blackout.

Scene 4   Streets of City

Lizzie is walking the streets of the city. She is in 19th century dress- homespun, half of her hair is cut off, the other half dyed red. Heavy boots. Even though it's night, she is very happy to be alive again.

Song: "New Lease on Life"

She realizes that she forgot to ask who the real murderer was. Soon she meets up with members of Rico's gang. Rather than thinking that she looks weird, they think she looks pretty cool. Her strange expressions and strange language (of the mill workers not too far away from the farm) seem to highlight the fact that she's not afraid to be different. She makes some good friends.

In this middle section of the play Lizzie experiences 20th century life. (Could be a number of miniscenes that highlight aspects of this life—show her surprise but delight.) First movie. First microwave. Cars. Airplanes. Telephone. She learns about AIDS, world wars, nuclear bombs, drugs, apathy towards education, desegregation, women's rights, etc. Her mind gets farther and farther away from helping Rico. She enjoys living, despite all its problems.

Pizza Shop- comic relief despite confrontation of two gangs.

Song: "Luigi's Pizzeria"

As Lizzie continues to make mistakes, have misunderstandings, most kids think that she is just trying to be different. Eventually one of her friends, Carla, corners her. "Why have you been avoiding staircases?" Lizzie finally confesses to Carla that she is from another century, but doesn't say anything about Rico.

Song: "Just My Imagination"

Scene 5   At the railroad trestle

Song: "My Gang's All I Got"

Rigas's gang and Rico's gang have a confrontation. Rigas tries to convince Lizzie to join his gang, and in the attempt, his girlfriend, Tanya, becomes angry with him for paying so much attention to Lizzie. Lizzie begins to realize that Rigas is the one who killed the teacher. He has no intention of turning himself in. He could care less if Rico gets blamed.

Song: "Hang With Us"

Song: "Seein' Wild Again"

Scene 6   Field trip to mills

After a couple of months Lizzie's class is brought to the mills on a field trip. The first room they go into is at the bottom of the stairs. As Ranger Dan, the tour guide talks, Lizzie, under her breath, corrects him when he makes mistakes. Her language has become more modern, still with a few words that show where she is from and when. Lizzie is the last student to leave this area. All of a sudden Rico appears. "Lizzie! What's takin' you so long?" Confused, Lizzie runs off to join the group.

The next stop is the weaving room. Ranger Dan tells how in the 1800's this room would have been filled with girls. When Lizzie looks it is filled with girls. She stays behind. None of the girls pay attention to her until she walks in front of Ruth. "Lizzie, ye be alive! How be ye alive?" All of the girls come running over. They are all dead. They all died in the mill: some from accidents, some from brown lung disease, some from the "kiss of death."

Song: "Tell Us Lizzie"

"Aren't you going to give your life back?" Ruth asks. Confused, Lizzie runs out. Lizzie runs into the museum room. She looks in a display case and sees something that had been hers. She turns around and sees herself in one of the pictures. She spins away and sees a plaster statue of herself. She's confused. She wants to live, but she wants to rectify this injustice, especially because she was never able to rectify the injustices suffered by the mill girls.

Song: Reprise "Mill Girls"

She grabs a shuttle and smashes the statue. Unknown to Lizzie, Rigas has been watching all this from the side of the room. She is out of control. She runs back to the stairwell. Rico tries to talk to her.

Song: Reprise "Up Against the Wall"

Lizzie doesn't want to hear Rico. She tells him to shut up. Rigas can not hear Rico. Instead, Rigas is attracted to her for her violence, not knowing where it is coming from. "You are bad . . . real bad." He makes advances toward her. She gets him to confess to firing the gun that killed the teacher. The ranger and other witnesses hear this. Rigas tries to move in closer. She tries to avoid him. Eventually he goes to grab and kiss her. She steps aside and he plunges down the five flights of stairs to his death. Rico comes back to life. Both he and Lizzie seem to be alive.

Song: Reprise "New Lease on Life " (*Rico and Lizzie together*)

Lights dim . . .

SAMPLE SCRIPT
Scene 1

SCENE 1: TEXTILE MILL, CITY IN NEW ENGLAND, IN THE 1800s

(Note: *The titles of songs and lyrics are the full texts of what students wrote, but not necessarily what was finally performed. The full text of "I'd Give My Soul for Silence" appears at the end of this scene. Only four lines from the song were actually sung on the tape.*)

"I'd Give My Soul for Silence:" mill girls
"That's Lizzie:" mill girls
"Weave a Fortune:" Ruth

We hear the sound of the looms while it is still dark. The lights come on and the mill girls begin to sing "I'd Give My Soul for Silence." The sound of the looms goes off during the song. When the song is done the sound of the looms comes back on.)

Overseer: *Get back to work!* (The sound of the looms continues softly in the background. The spotlight goes on Lizzie and Ruth.)

Lizzie: *Back to work, eh? That's all we do is work. Me be gettin' so angry at Mr. Hamilton. Nothin' we do seems good enough for him.*

Ruth: *I know what you mean. But don't you be thinkin' of doin' anything you'll regret later, eh?*

Lizzie: *What do you think I'd do?* (sarcastically)

Ruth: *I know you, Lizzie. Know you be goin' to play some kinda trick . . .* (pause) *. . . oh damn!*

Lizzie: *Hard day, eh?*

Overseer: *Hard day? Lord, none of you girls knows what a hard day is. Ruth! What are you trying to hide? You're doing that all wrong! Can't you get anything straight? Straighten that cloth . . . get those warp threads tight. Look at this . . . your weaver's knot ain't holdin' . . . If you continue to do this incorrectly I'm going to have to dismiss you, hear?*

Ruth: *I-I-I'm sorry Mr. Hamilton. Puttin' me on six looms is harder than tryin' to git milk from a dried up old cow. I'll try to keep it all straight.* (Overseer mumbles under his breath and walks away.) *He's right. Ain't nothin' I do is right. These threads are so confusin' . . .* (Ruth starts to cry. Lizzie, who has heard the entire conversation, walks over to Ruth.)

Lizzie: (comforting) *It's all right, Ruth! Now, you better stop that blubberin' or your bolt will be ruined for good, eh.* (Pause.) *The only thing confusin' is Mr. Hamilton's expectations. I expect I kin unconfuse him. Here, let* *me help git these threads straightened for you.* (Lizzie helps Ruth fix her material. The overseer walks over again to check Ruth's loom.)

Overseer: (to Ruth) *Sorry, dear, it's just that your work isn't as good as your looks.* (He pats Ruth on her butt. As the overseer walks away, Lizzie pushes a bucket out into the aisle that trips him.) *Damn you girl! You're the blister on my heel . . .*

Ruth: *That weren't Lizzie's fault, sir! That was a mistake.*

Lizzie: *The only mistake was him talkin' to you like that. Creation! If the Lord don't git even.* (to the overseer) *Lord knows you ain't got no right to talk to her like that. An' you sure ain't got no right to touch . . .*

Overseer: (quickly jumps in) *Touch? What I can touch is your weekly pay. You watch it missy, or you'll be losin' more than a few warp threads.*

Lizzie: *You bein' the only thing that's warped around here . . .* (said under her breath at the overseer).

ALL: Lizzie!

Ruth: *Whatta ya think you be doin', Lizzie? You nearly lost your pay too.*

(Overseer walks away.) *I can't believe he don't blacklist you . . .*

Lizzie: *Ruth, you be seein' anyone who works eight looms alone blacklisted? I ain't afraid of no overseer. You gotta be tough here . . .*

  Song: *"That's Lizzie"*

The supper bell rings.

Ruth: *Creation! These warp threads keep snappin' . . . An' if only I could block out this wretched noise . . .*

Lizzie: (Yelling over the looms. She finishes hers, then . . .) *You want I should help you, Ruth? We'll have to work fast, eh?*

Ruth: *It ain't your fault my threads keep snappin'.*

Lizzie: *Well, it ain't your fault neither.*

  Song: *"Weave a Fortune"*

Lizzie: *Come on, Ruth, we'll have to work fast, eh?*

Ruth: *Lizzie, you be so good to all us newer girls, 'specially me. You be the only friend I got. don't trouble your-self more now.* (The supper bell rings.) *I have to go. I'm obliged to set the table for supper.*

Lizzie: *You go. I'll finish it off for ye. I'll be there in the flash of a lightnin' bolt.*

Ruth: *Lizzie, you promise me, you ain't be slidin' down no bannister agin, ey? You be the only friend I got here. Cross your heart?*

Lizzie: *Cross my heart and hope to die on the Sabbath if I do. Now don't you fright yourself, Ruth.* (Lizzie has her fingers crossed behind her back.)

Ruth: *I don't want to see you hurt, eh.*

Lizzie: (Continues to work until she finishes Ruth's bolt. In her rush though she catches her hair in the loom. She must cut off a huge hunk of hair to release the hold—or be scalped. When she falls, she lands in a bucket of red dye. All this trouble hardly fazes her.) *Damnation all to hell! I be really late.* (Lizzie runs to the stairway and leaps onto the bannister. She misses, plunging 5 flights to her death.)

"I'd Give My Soul for Silence"
by Jeannemarie

(Note: Only the first four lines, highlighted in bold, were actually sung during the performance, and the title was changed to "Mill Girls" for the play and the taping.)

Mill girls run as fast as fire
The bell tolls loud, hard work its desire.

Chrous: The shuttle flies from end to end
Weave and spin, weave and spin
Break and mend, break and mend
I'd give my soul for silence.

The giant beasts roar like thunder on the plain
The cotton dust flies like furious rain.

Chorus

Their fingers twirl, their feet are sore
The looms don't rest, just cry for more.

Chorus

Day after day the bell is rung
Their only wish, that day is done.

Chorus

The machines demand total compliance
I'd give my soul for silence.

SAMPLE SCRIPT
Scene 2

SCENE 2: HIGH SCHOOL HISTORY CLASS— CITY IN NEW ENGLAND, IN THE 1990s

(*Note: The titles of songs and lyrics are the full texts of what students wrote, but not necessarily what was finally performed.*)

"Reached the Breakin' Point ," Rap song from opposing gang members

This is a violent class—filled with the members of two rival gangs: the Pounders, led by Rico, and the RIPS, led by Rigas, dressed in black. They are really bad. Rico and the Pounders dress in red. They are tough, but not bad. They've all led terrible lives, hate each other, and stick up for gang members like they are their only family. In most cases, they are. This scene needs to develop Rico and Rigas, why they hate each other, and that Rico is really a more endearing character. Rigas comes to class intent on shooting one of Rico's gang members.

Lights are on the teacher. Rest of the stage is in semi-darkness. We can see that the students are really not paying attention. Focus is on the teacher for the audience anyway.

Teacher: (flatly) *The weaving rooms of these mills—excuse me, does anyone recall what revolution we were discussing yesterday?*

Student: *The American Revolution?*

Student: *Nah—he's talkin' about the revolution on 49th St. last year . . .*

Teacher: *That's right—we were discussing the Industrial Revolution. Our city played a major role during this extraordinary time in our history. And I guess, in a remote kind of way, one could tie in the American Revolution with the Industrial Revolution. Both were dangerous. The weaving rooms of the mill, right next door here for instance, were very dangerous places. The young women who worked on the looms were often hurt or even died as a result of working in these factories. As a matter of fact one young woman was killed in this very mill, but not in the weave room. She actually fell 5 stories when she tried to slide down the bannister of the stairwell. You can well imagine, with little knowledge of surgical procedures in those days, and just about every bone in her body smashed, she died two days later.*

Rigas: *And today's the day I'm gonna smash every bone in Tengo's body. He ain't gonna get away with it.*

Teacher: *Her name, I believe, was Lizzie . . . and the rumor is that her ghost still haunts the mill today, looking for a soul to share . . .*

Rigas: *I'll share his soul all right. They'll have to scrape his remains off the sidewalk to share with the worms that'll be crawlin' through his teeth . . .*

Rico: *Hey punk—who are you talkin' to? You got a Sprint line to your daddy in prison?*

Rigas: *At least I got an old man. He didn't split like yours when he saw your ugly face. Is that a requirement for the Pounders, ugly as dogfish and ears like Dumbo the elephant?*

Rico: *And requirements for the RIPS is just a BIG MOUTH. I heard you been mouthin' off about killin' Tengo.*

Rigas: *That jus' proves you got elephant ears. I ain't said nothin' to nobody. The only talkin' I'll be doin' is with the piece in my pocket.* (Rigas fingers something in his pocket, pulling out only enough so the butt end of a gun is showing.)

Rico: *You're trippin', Rigas. At least the Pounders would have the sense to settle a little bad fix in a more humane way—an eye for an eye—as the almanac says.*

Rigas: *Rico, you are so friggin' stupid. An "eye for an eye" is from Bartlett's F-a-m-i-l-y* (he drags the word out and emphasizes every syllable) *Quotations. An' I believe in the same thing. For givin' me a bad trip—a waste of my precious time here on earth—I am going to waste Tengo. TAKE HIM DOWN, for those of you who ain't real bright.*

Rigas's Gang Member: *Yo, Rigas. I got it. Shoot him . . ..we need some excitement around here. There's nothin' happenin' . . .*

"Reached the Breakin' Point" (various gang members take turns)

Teacher: *What's going on? What's with you two?* (Rico and Rigas).

Rigas: (loud whisper, neither one paying attention to the teacher) *You watch your mouth, Rico, or you're the one that's gonna get hurt.*

Rico: *Use your ugly head for once, Rigas. You can't get away with shootin' someone in front of 30 witnesses. You'll end up in the slammer with your old man—or maybe that's what you're lookin' for—a family reunion. An' I'll have to take you down. I can't let you go hurtin' no Pounders.*

Rigas: *Take me down? YOU take ME down. Is that a promise or a threat?*

Teacher: *Boys, boys. The only taking down is going to be the three of us to the office if you don't stop the frantic whispering and start taking some notes. Remember, we have a field trip coming up and you have a test on all of this on Friday.*

Rigas: (staring at Rico) *Here's a TEST for you. Who's the most powerful man in this room right now? A Mr. Hamilton, B Rico, or C ME ?* (Rigas stands and starts to pull the gun from his pocket as he approaches Tengo from behind. Rico leaps up and dives on top of him.)

Teacher: *Boys! Boys! We adhere to a strict code of discipline. In the hall. In the hall. The two of you. NOW!*

All three of them go out into the hall (could be offstage). We hear Rico trying to talk Rigas out of the gun. The teacher doesn't even know he has one. In some kind of struggle—off stage—the teacher is shot while Rico struggles to get the gun away from Rigas. They both run back into the classroom, Rico holding the gun but claiming he was just trying to get it away from Rigas. His gang members tell him to get out—get away . . . Lights go down with Rico running.

"Reached the Breakin' Point"
by Jen, Kevin, Sam, and Jeremy

(*Note: Gang members from Pounders and Rips take turns singing parts. All gang members sing chorus together.*)

My father left when I was young
Mama's always sick
If I had my choice of lives, this ain't what I'd pick

> Chorus: My father left me
> My mama was shot
> I live in a ghetto
> My gang's all I got
> Now I'm livin' on my own
> Where the drugs flow faster than blood

> This mornin' on my way to school
> A guy tried to sell me crack
> But I got enough problems in life
> Don't need no monkey on my back

A kid at school was shot last week
Last month a chick was raped
My turn is proble' comin' soon
There just ain't no escape.

> Chorus

> I wish my life was better
> But there ain't much I can do
> Can't afford to go to college
> An' high school's almost through.

I got a job at Quickie Mart
Five bucks an hour ain't much
But it pays some bills and groceries
And it buys my mama's scotch.

> Chorus

> I'll never be nothin' important
> Just a person who lived and died
> And nothin' will ever change that
> No matter how hard I've cried.

A RIVER RAN WILD, by Lynne Cherry

"They came down from the mountain, and at the river's edge they knelt to quench their thirst with its clear water. Pebbles shone up from the bottom. 'Let us settle by this river,' said the chief of the native people. He named the rive Nash-a-way—River with the Pebbled Bottom."

Centuries later the Nash-a-way River was declared ecologically dead, the shiny pebbles and clear water smothered by years of waste dumped into the river by textile mills.

Through beautiful illustrations and descriptive words Lynne Cherry tells us the history of the Nashua River. *A River Ran Wild* is not just a picture book. It is not just a report on the environmental history of the Nashua River. It is a careful combination of detailed illustrations and facts, woven together in a story that has appeal for all ages.

The clever, beautiful illustrations bordering the pages give the reader a better idea of the times and the place in which this story takes place. The book helps us understand and respect the environment. It inspires us to save our lakes and rivers while we still can.

A River Ran Wild is the story of an Algonquin tribe's home. It is the story of industry and progress begun by the colonists. It is the story of terrible pollution and disrespect for the environment, causing the death of a beautiful resource. It is the story of the inspiring salvation of this resource by ordinary people who love the environment. It is the story of the Nash-a-way, the river with the pebbled bottom.

Review by Kristen

THE LORAX, by Dr. Seuss

"Protect it from the axes that hack. Then the Lorax and all of his friends may come back."

When you first hear the words "picture book," you relate them to children, but the reality is that they often address serious topics that even older students can enjoy.

The Lorax is a delightful story that makes a serious point: by being too greedy we can lose everything. The rhythm, combined with colorful pictures, tells us that if you really love something, save it! Dr. Seuss lets us step into his world of Truffula trees and the Brown Bar-ba-loots, led by the wise old Lorax. Their enemy, the Once-ler, narrates the message about planet earth. Once there were crystal waters and clear skies, now tarnished with pollutants. Now certain animals and plants can only be read about—or seen in science books. Like the Truffula Trees, the Brown Bar-ba-loots, the Humming-Fish, and the Swomee-Swans, we have our own animals and plants in jeopardy. Dr. Seuss wants us to care for and respect the world around us.

Review by Casey, Anne, and Michele

"Mill Girls"

Written by Jeannemarie
Sung by mill girls

Lyrics: *Mill girls! Run as fast as fire!*
The bell tolls loud, hard work its desire!
The giant beast roars like thunder on the plain.
The cotton dust flies like furious rain.

"That's Lizzie"

Written by Tara and Kate
Sung by Tara, Jeannemarie, Kate

Lyrics: *Lizzie, that girl, she's our friend, she's our pal*
Makin' life tolerable in the mill on the canal
She always talks back, not afraid to fight
While we weave meekly, spin and weave in fright

That's Lizzie, crazy as can be, that's Lizzie
Always livin' life free, that's Lizzie, crazy as crazy can be

On the boardinghouse roof where she often hides
Talkin' with the stars, takin' life in strides
Slidin' down the bannister to get to supper first
Never thinkin' of danger, never fearin' the worst.

That's Lizzie, crazy as can be, that's Lizzie . . . Always
livin' life free, that's Lizzie, crazy as crazy can be.

"Weave a Fortune"

Written by Laura
Sung by Sarah

Lyrics: *I wanted. . . to weave a fortune, turn riches out of rags*
But you'll never be rich if there's a hitch in your stitch
    and your money bag's strikin' snags
I wanted to. . . weave a fortune, turn riches out of rags
But you'll never be rich if there's a hitch in your stitch
    and your money bag's strikin' snags
First I milk the cows, then I feed the sows
As the day goes on I have to work the farm
I wish this day to end, as the night's my only friend
I wanted to weave a fortune, turn riches out of rags
But you'll never be rich if there's a hitch in your stitch
    and your money bag's strikin' snags
I wanted to weave . . .

"Reached the Breaking Point"

Written and Sung by 7K ("The Pounders" and "The RIPS")

"Up Against the Wall"

Written by Alyssa and Julie
Sung by Matt

Lyrics: *I sometimes wonder . . . what has happened to me.*
I was left alone, dropped on the street.
Just eight years old, left to fend for myself.
Nothin' really mattered, not even life itself.
This, this is my life, this is how it goes.
When you live the way that I do,
You get used to the blows.
When somethin's goin' down, someone's got to fall.
This is my life, up against the wall.

"Switch"

Written by Rachel and Dave Ervin
Sung by Rachel (Lizzie) and Matt (Rico)

Lyrics: *Switch . . . (Lizzie)*
Switch? (Rico)
Switch.
Right.
Listen, I'd be there; you'd be here. Or would I be here?
and you'd be there? Well, it doesn't really matter which
is which. . . 'cause we'd just switch.
Wait, wait. . .this is confusing! I don't   understand. . .
there's gotta be a hitch! Great! Great! This really ain't
amusing!
You got a ghost of a chance, if we just switch.
   How?
If you simply disappear, then I'd be there and you'd be
here. It just requires your consent. . . then I'll prove
you're innocent!
Did you say, simply disappear? . . .and you'd be here
instead?
That's what I said.
Simply disappear?
You see. . . I'm dead.
   DEAD?
   Dead!

Right. . .
Well, I started here, ended there. Jumped for the stairs,
but landed on air. I took a header, headed for my
head. . . so now, I'm dead.
Whoa! Whoa! I don't comprehend it. It simply don't jive.
You landed on your head! No! No! I cannot defend it.
Gotta ghost of a chance if you're dead.
What?
You gotta believe me; I'm tellin' you it's true. Here's
what we do. 'Cause if somebody dies. . . It's the perfect
disguise! Conk off! Kick off! Pipe off! Pop off! Shove off!
Shut off! Shuffle off! Drop off! What do you say?
What do I say?
What do you say?
No way!

"New Lease on Life"

Written and Sung by Rachel

Lyrics: *Each step takes me somewhere new;*
each breath makes me stronger.
Each pulse brings me closer to, the life I knew.
Can this be true?
A moment to live longer!
A new lease on life. Can this be true?
My head is spinning!
A new lease on life. The morning dew, a new beginning.
A chance to breathe and sigh, to laugh and cry,
to wonder why.
A chance to dance again!
A new lease. . . on life.
. . . on life. . . a new lease.

"Luigi's Pizzeria"

Written by Anne
Sung by Jamie (Luigi) and Kiki (Mama Guito)

Lyrics: *When I was a boy, I learned from a book.*
And thus I became, a stupendous cook.
More like stupid, Luigi.
I sell by the pan, I sell by the slice.
I pile on the cheese to make it taste nice.
I'm the best of the best, the creme de la crop.

> *My pizza is crisp, . . .*
> > *But it all tastes like slop.*
> *I mop all the floors; I spit clean the dish.*
> *And I find connoisseurs for the anchovy fish.*
> *We got sausage, pepperoni, fish that's not too bony.*
> *Mark my testimony, 'cause we got baloney.*
> *If that is too fatty, try our chicken pattie.*
> *Maybe I could toss-a hunk of kielbasa*
> > *in the pizza sauce-a*
>
> *Mushrooms and tomatoes, onions, fried potatoes*
> *Cooked up while you wait-o, let us fill your plat-o*
> *Sizzle up a treat-a, made for you to eat up*
> *Got them on their knees for pizza jubilee*
>
> *We've got meatballs and spaghetti,*
> > *mushrooms and spaghetti,*
> *Meatloaf and spaghetti, olives and spaghetti,*
> > *peppers and spaghetti,*
> *Spaghetti and spaghetti . . .*
>
> *Such fine Italian treats ya, eat at Luigi's pizza*
> *Nobody compete's with great Luigi's pizza,*
> *Always aimed to pleats (please) so,*
> > *sit down in your seats at. . . Luigi's Pizza.*

"Just My Imagination"

Written and Sung by Katherine

Lyrics: *Sometimes I wonder if anything is real*
> *The truth doesn't seem like reality.*
> *Is it just my imagination again?*
> *What about when automobiles seemed*
> > *so intriguing?*
> *What about when movies appeared*
> > *awfully enchanting?*
> *Am I crazy? The truth is getting hazy.*
> *Then there's the time, when the cut never bled.*
> *Then there's the time, when the staircase*
> > *she fled.*
> *Am I going mad? This is really getting bad.*
> > *Sometimes I wonder, if anything is real.*
> *The truth doesn't seem like reality.*
> *Is it just my imagination again?*

"My Gang's All I Got"

Written and Sung by Sam

Lyrics: *When I was a baby, dropped on my head.*
And now I'm lucky that I'm messed up, not dead.
My mother left me, my father was shot
Livin' in the ghetto and my gang's all I got.
Now I'm livin' in a slum, where the drugs
    flow faster than blood. Don't ya know?

My best friend, locked up in the slammer.
Hit a policeman with an old sledgehammer.
I guess I'd be okay if someone paid attention to . . .
    someone gave some lovin' to . . .
    someone didn't turn their back on me.

"Hang with Us"

Written and Sung by 7L "The RIPS"

Lyrics: *Lizzie girl, why don't we hang?*
We could stick like glue, you scorchin' thing.
We could show to you, a better time,
'Cause if you don't come Lizzie,
    it would be a crime.
So hang with us, Lizzie, hang with us . .
    or just hang.
Lizzie girl, why aren't you with us?
We could steal a car, hijack a bus. . .
We could go real far, or go real fast,
So just come with us Lizzie, we'll have a blast.
So hang with us, Lizzie, hang with us. . .
    or just hang.

Make up your mind, Lizzie; do you want
    to be tough?
You can hang with the RIPS; you've got the stuff.
But say you're not with us and you've
    said enough.
You'll be finding that your lifestyle
    could be gettin' a little rough.
So hang with us, Lizzie, hang with us. . .
    or just hang.

"Seein' Wild Again"

Written by Casey

Sung by Casey (Tanya) and Rory (Rigas)

Lyrics: *She's a wild one, Rigas.*
　　　　That's it. You got it.
Another girl to shame.
　　　　Better watch your mouth. You're goin' down.
She's a wild one, Rigas . . .
　　　　You only got what was comin' to you.
Another colt to tame.
　　　　Better watch your head. Your goin' down.
Well I was wild once, Rigas . . .
　　　　I'm warnin' you Tanya . . .
Remember me back then?
　　　　Tellin' you, your threats
　　　　will come back round.
I was wild once, Rigas; and you'll be seein' wild
again. You can take me down, Rigas. Break my
heart just like before. You can close your cage
around me, but I won't take it, . . .
No, I won't take it . . . No I won't take it anymore.

"Tell Us Lizzie"

Written by 7M

Sung by Rachel, Jeanne, Larisa, Tara

Lyrics: *It was getting mighty busy . . .*
　　　　We were workin' up a tizzie
　　　　　　Tell us Lizzie! Tell us Lizzie! Tell us Lizzie!
　　　　Got lifted high up in the room, when my hair
　　　　　　caught in the loom.
　　　　　　'Cause it was frizzy!
　　　　　　Tell us Lizzie! Tell us Lizzie!
　　　　As I lifted even higher. . .
　　　　　　and she knew that she might die. . .
　　　　or crack my head against some lead. . .
　　　　　　or get her neck caught in a wire!
　　　　I reached down into my apron
　　　　　　for some scissors. . .
　　　　　　or a plier!

and I cut my hair!
> *She cut her hair!*
Fell down from there!
> *Fell down from there!*
My brain was kinda fizzy and my stomach
> *really "quizzy,"*
> *Tell us Lizzie! Tell us Lizzie! Tell us Lizzie!*
My feet hit on the floor, but my head fell even more
> *'Cause she was dizzy*
> *Tell us Lizzie! Tell us Lizzie!*
I was falling to a bucket. . .
> *That is awfully nasty luck. . .*
It made my head turn bloody red!
> *If you'd only tried to duck it!*
I reached down into my apron
> *for some bandages to tuck it,*
> *but to no avail!*
> *To no avail?*
My face fell pale. . .
> *A sad, sad tale!*

"Mill Girls" (reprise)

"Up Against the Wall" (reprise)

Sung by Joshua

Mill Girls!

O.R.M.S. 7th Grade

c. 1994

Appendix S
MUSICAL ARRANGEMENT: "MILL GIRLS" (*continued*)

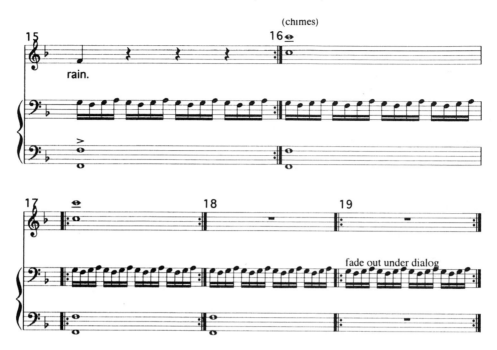

Up Against the Wall

O.R.M.S. 7th Grade

c. 1994

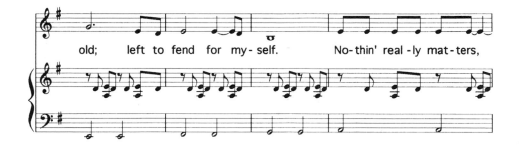

old; left to fend for my-self. No-thin' real-ly mat-ters,

not e-ven life it-self.

This, this is my life. . This is how it

goes. . . When you live the way that

Appendix S
MUSICAL ARRANGEMENT: "UP AGAINST THE WALL" (*continued*)